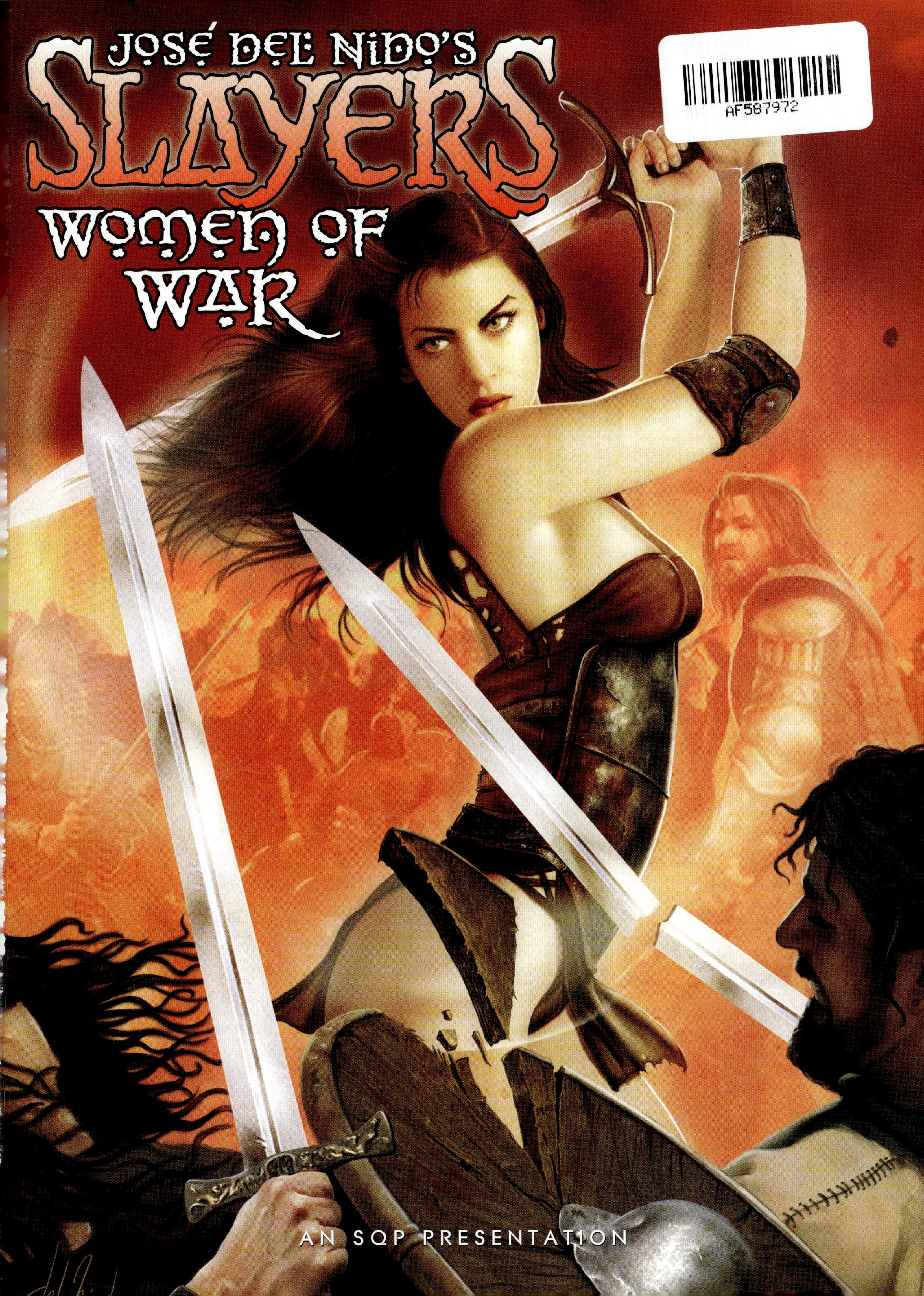
JOSÉ DEL NIDO'S
SLAYERS
WOMEN OF WAR
AN SQP PRESENTATION

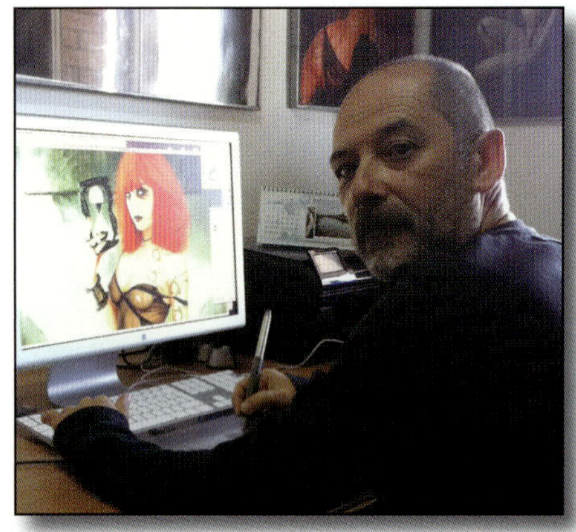

ABOUT THE ARTIST:

José del Nido was born in Barcelona, Spain. He has worked as an illustrator for more than 30 years. From the beginning, he has mastered almost all the techniques of the media: oil, acrilics, watercolor, airbrush, etc. In the last few years he's incorported those talents into the digital realm, and uses Corel Painter software.

He's worked for many publishing houses and advertising agencies from all over the world, such as Bastei, Euraeditoriale, Norma, Planeta, Grupo Zeta among others.

His powerful illustrations have been created for covers to books, comics, videogames, magazines, posters and puzzles. Jhon Sinclair, Torn, Vampire, Maddrax, Scorpio, Lanciostory, Two Worlds, are a few examples.

In 2003 MG Publishing/SQP Art Books edited a book with one hundred of his illustrations, called ***The Art of José del Nido***.

In October 2007, ***The Art Scene International*** magazine, dedicated the cover article to his work.

With the illustrator and friend J.R. Domingo, he has published two fantasy art books, ***Atrvm*** and ***Fatvm***.

Presently, he works from Sant Joan Despí, a place near Barcelona, where he maintains a studio.

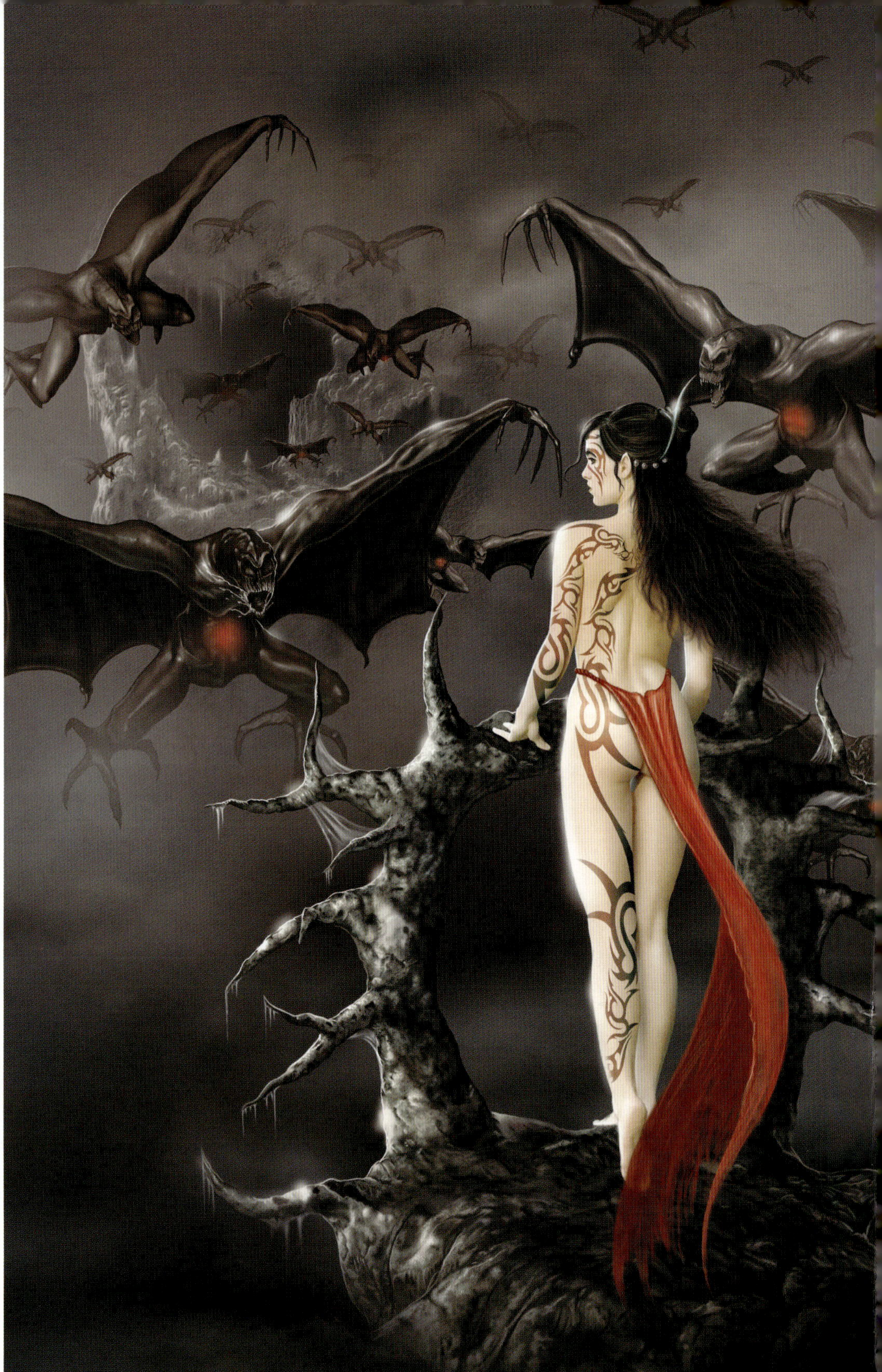

For the latest works and information about José, go to www.josedelnido.com

Slayers - Women of War
by Jose' del Nido

Book design by Grassy Knoll Studios.

Published by SQP Inc.
PO Box 248 - Columbus NJ 08022
Sal Quartuccio & Bob Keenan - Publishers

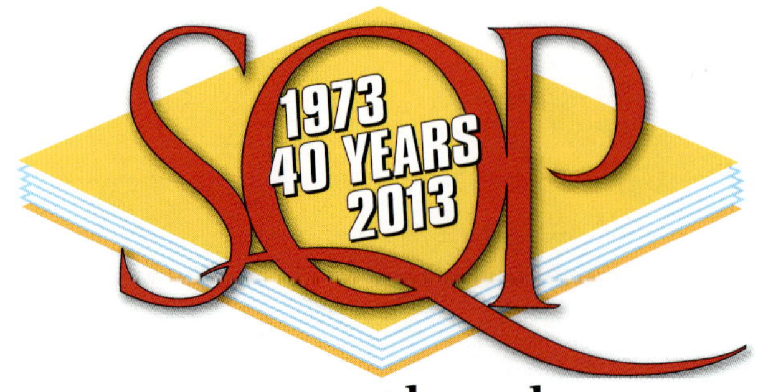

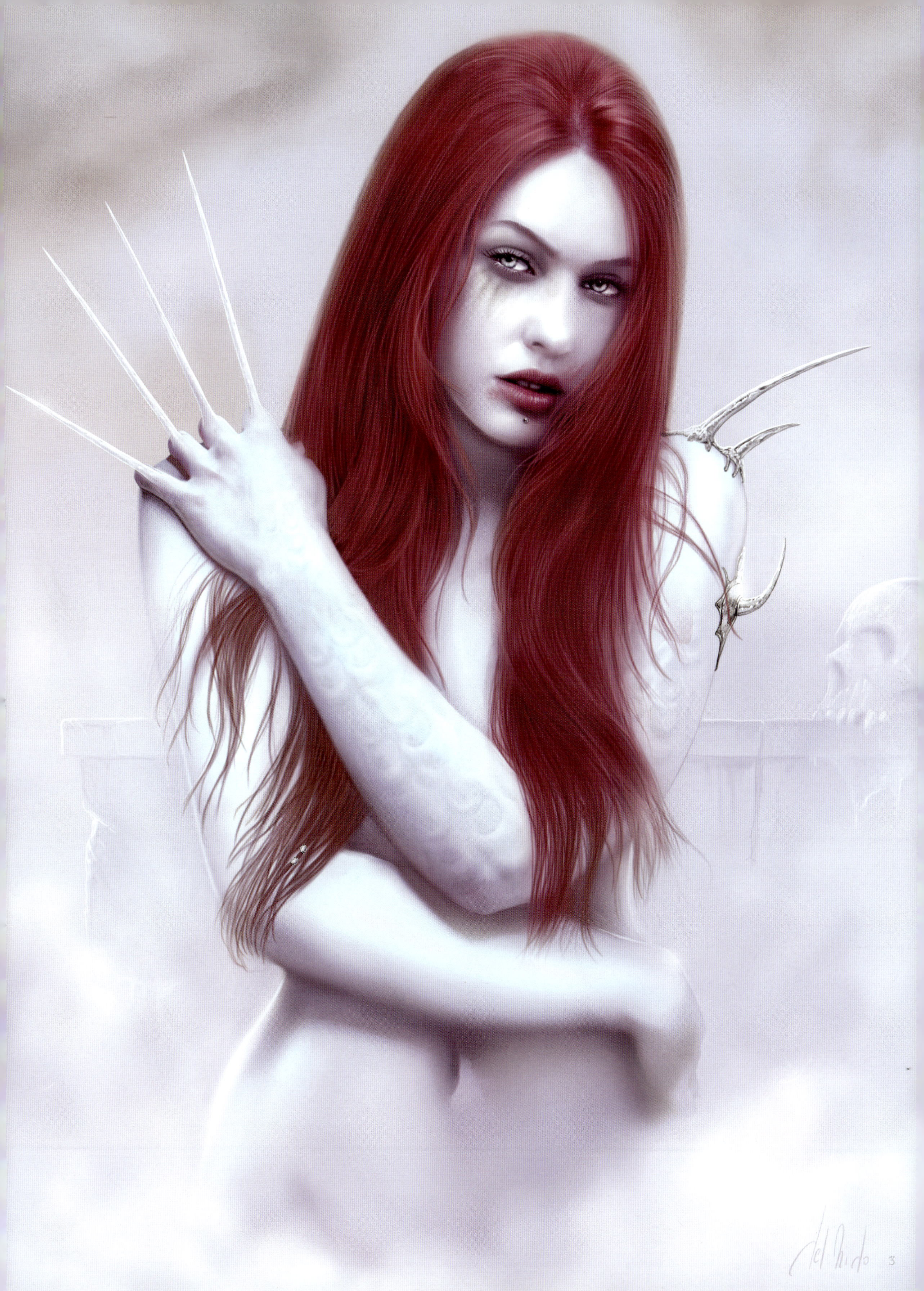

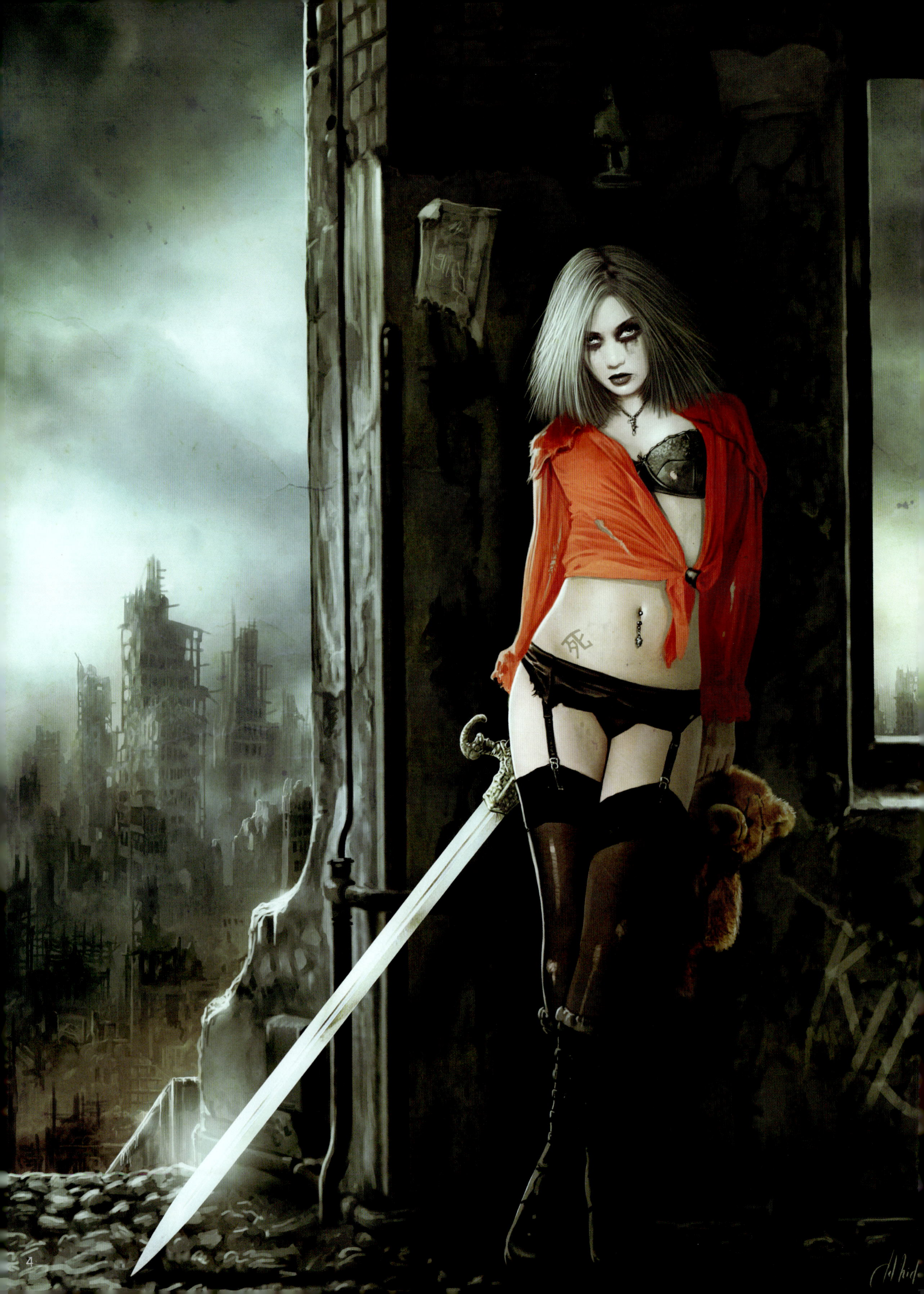

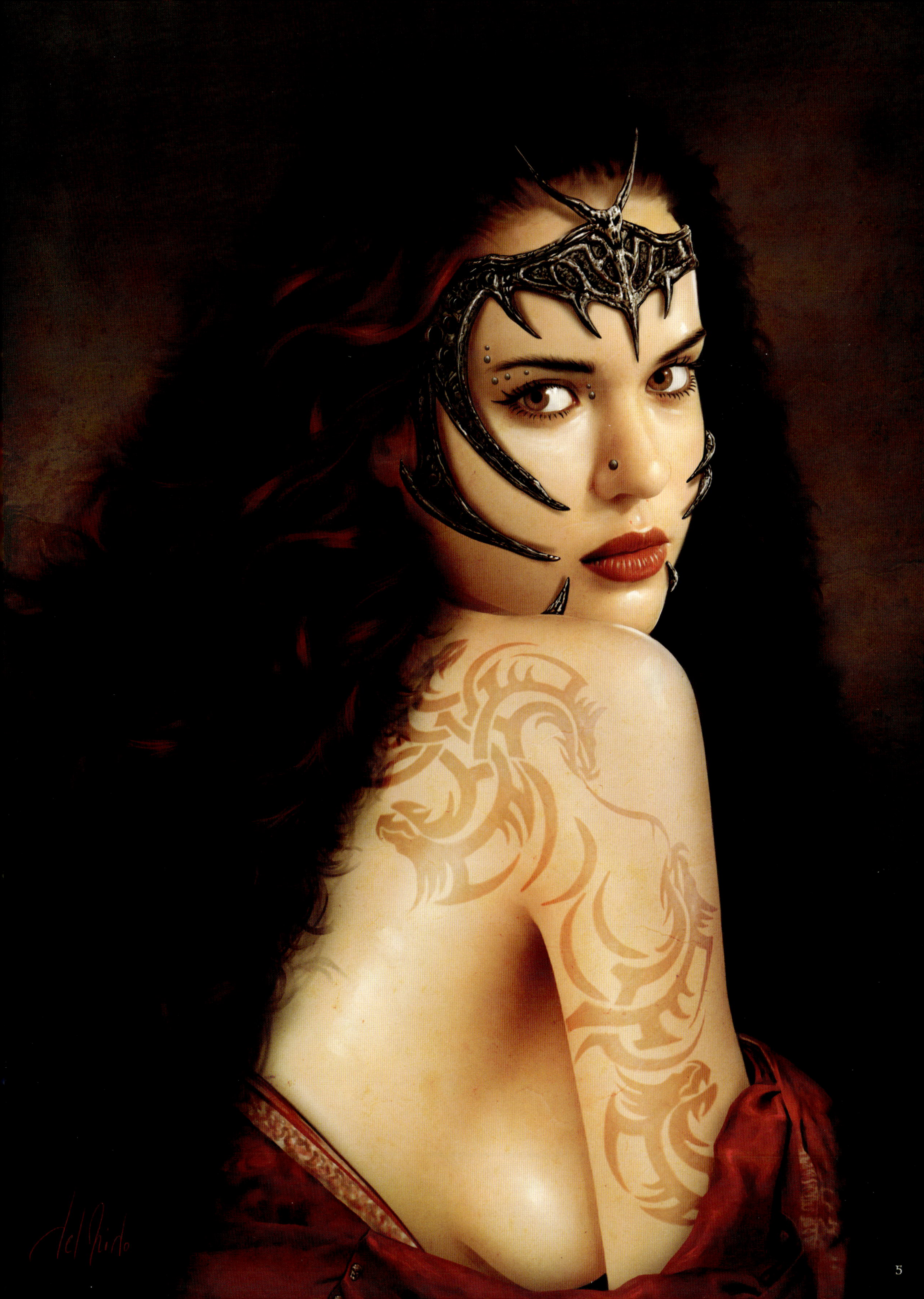

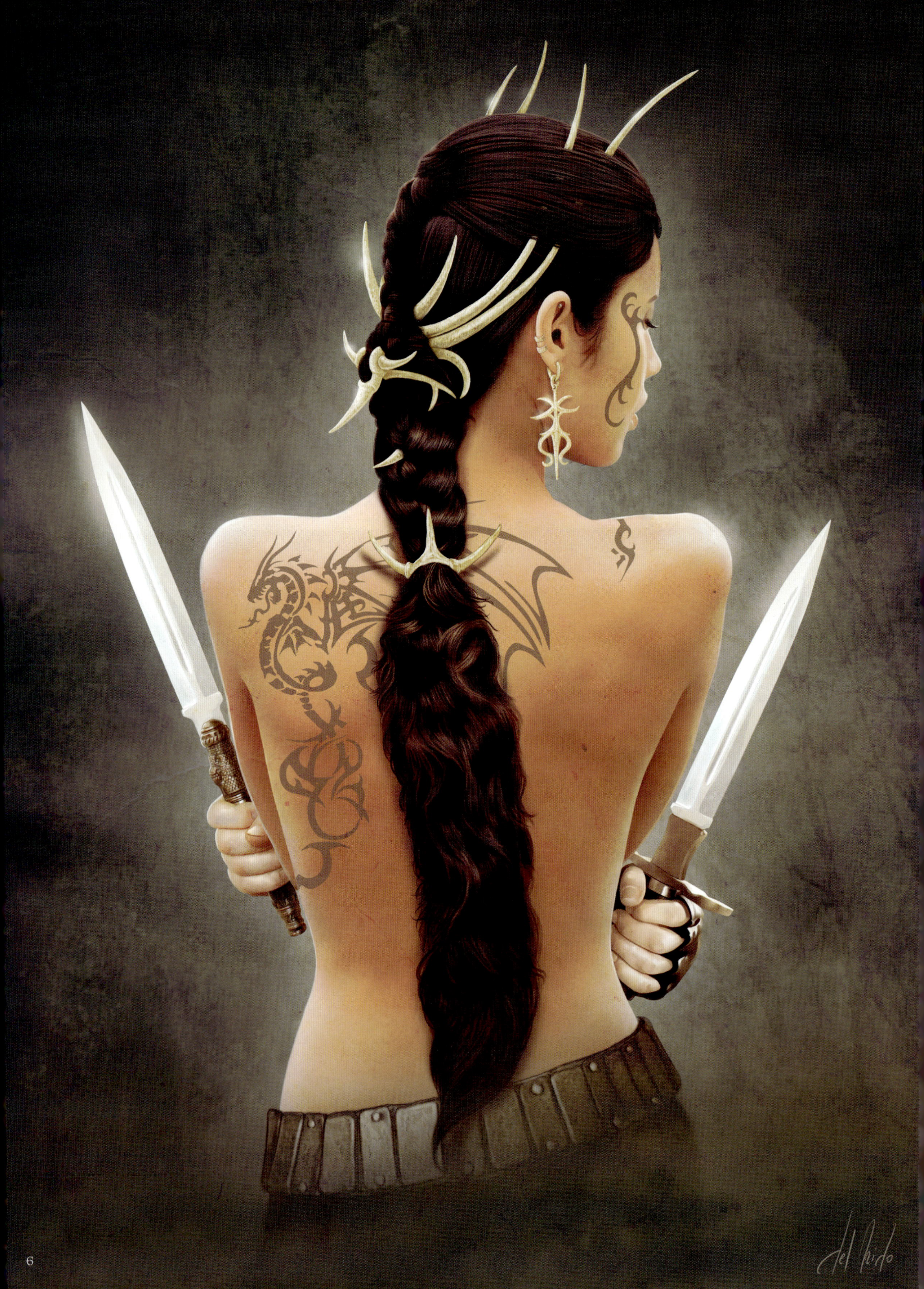

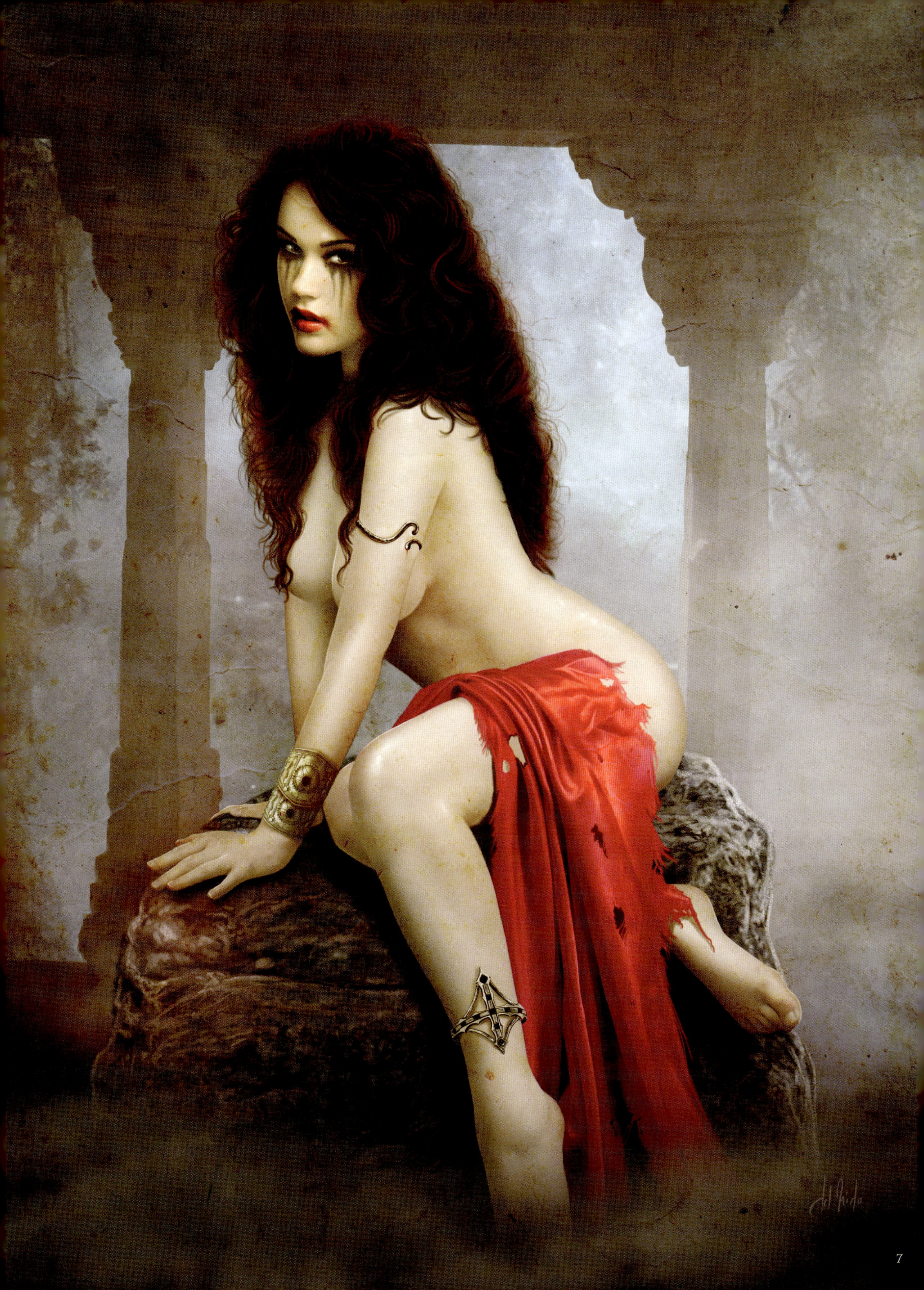

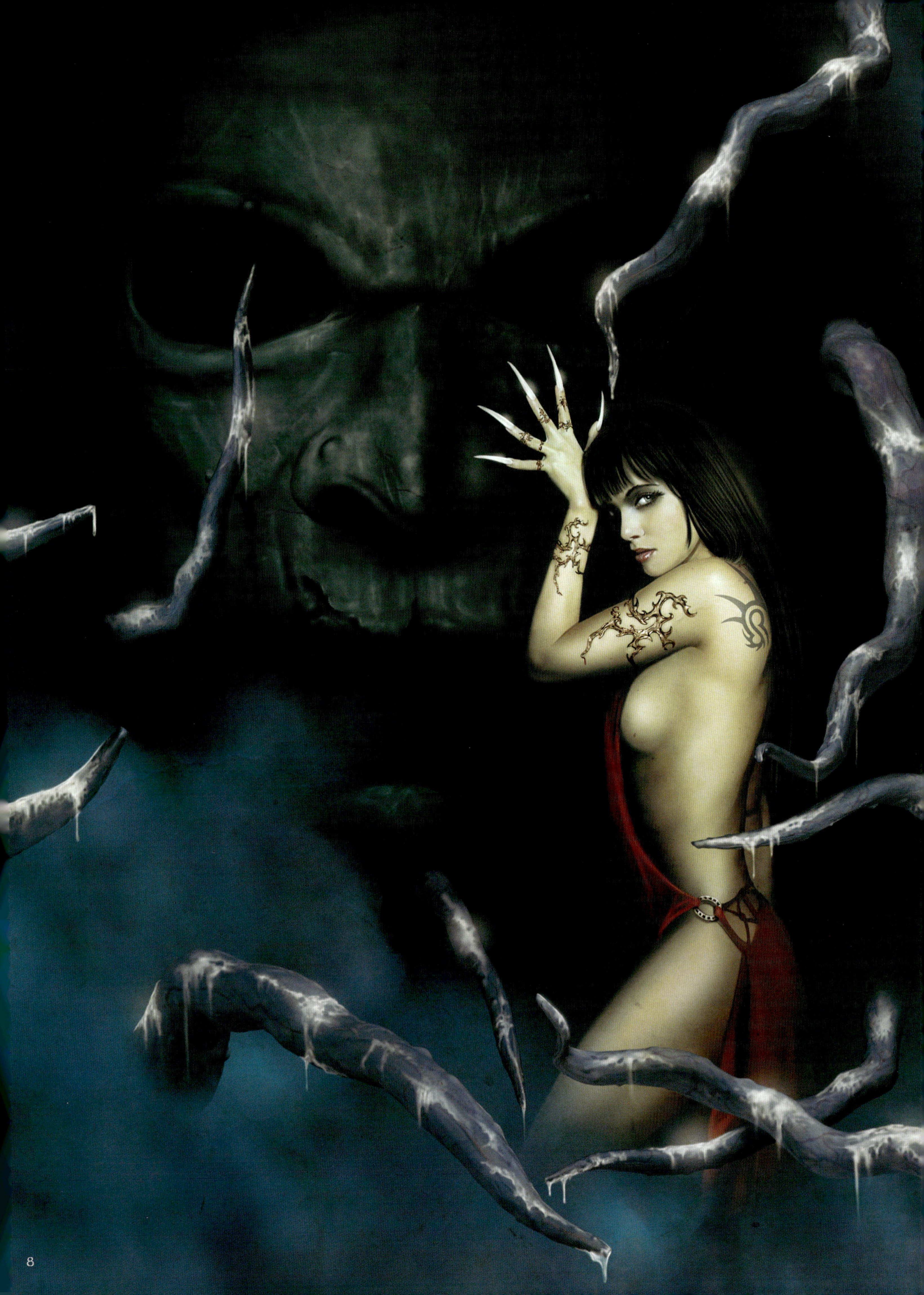

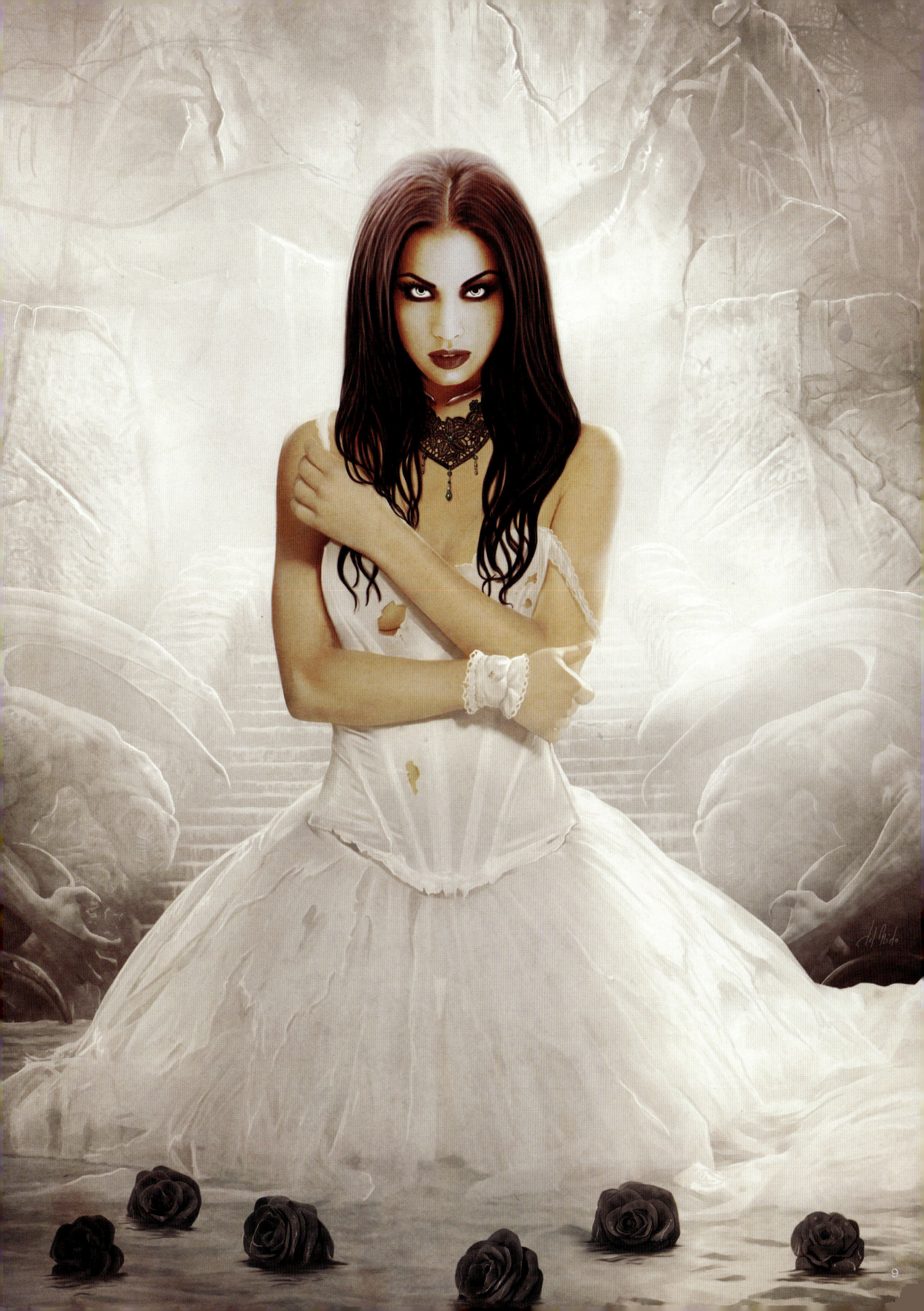

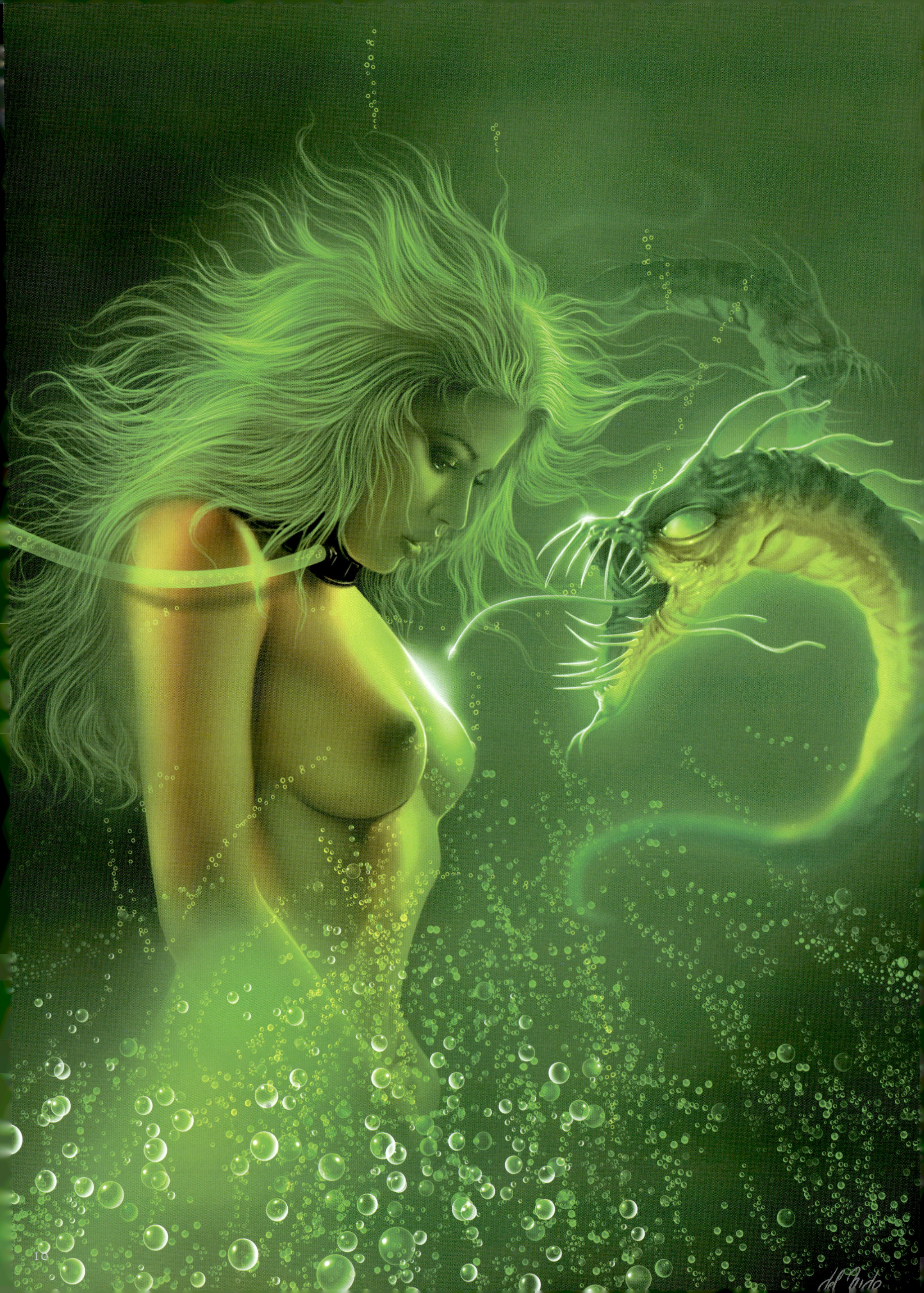

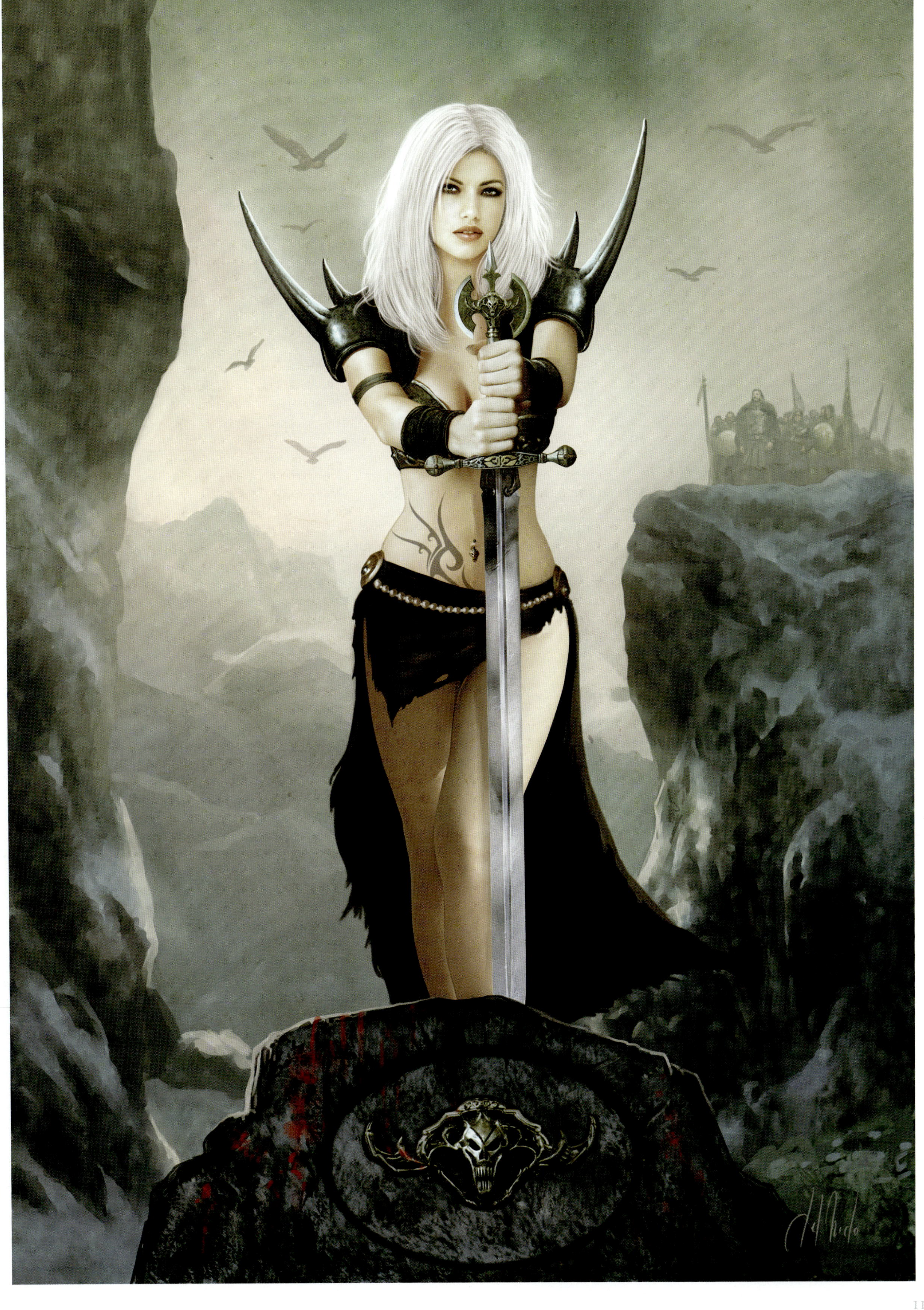

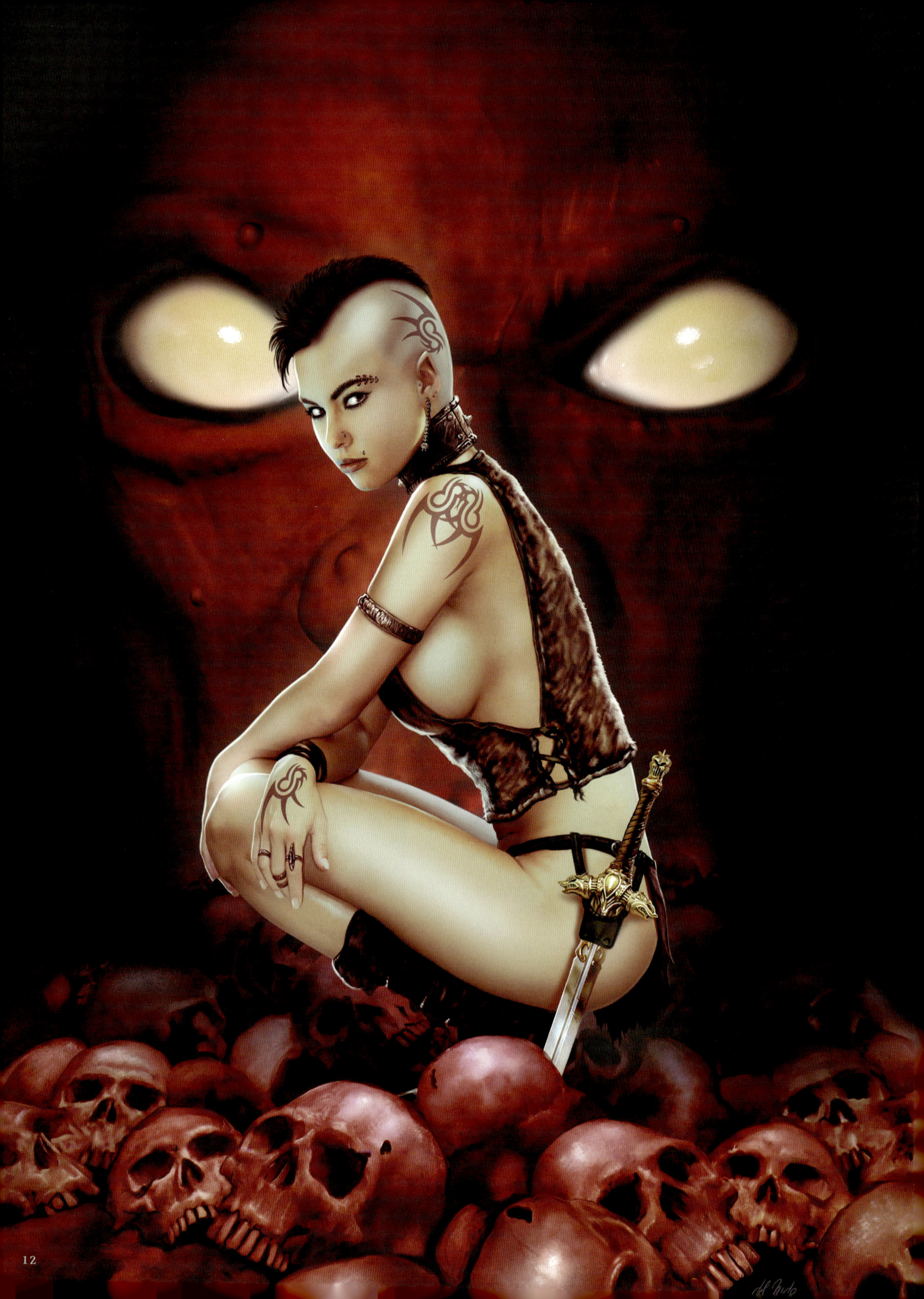

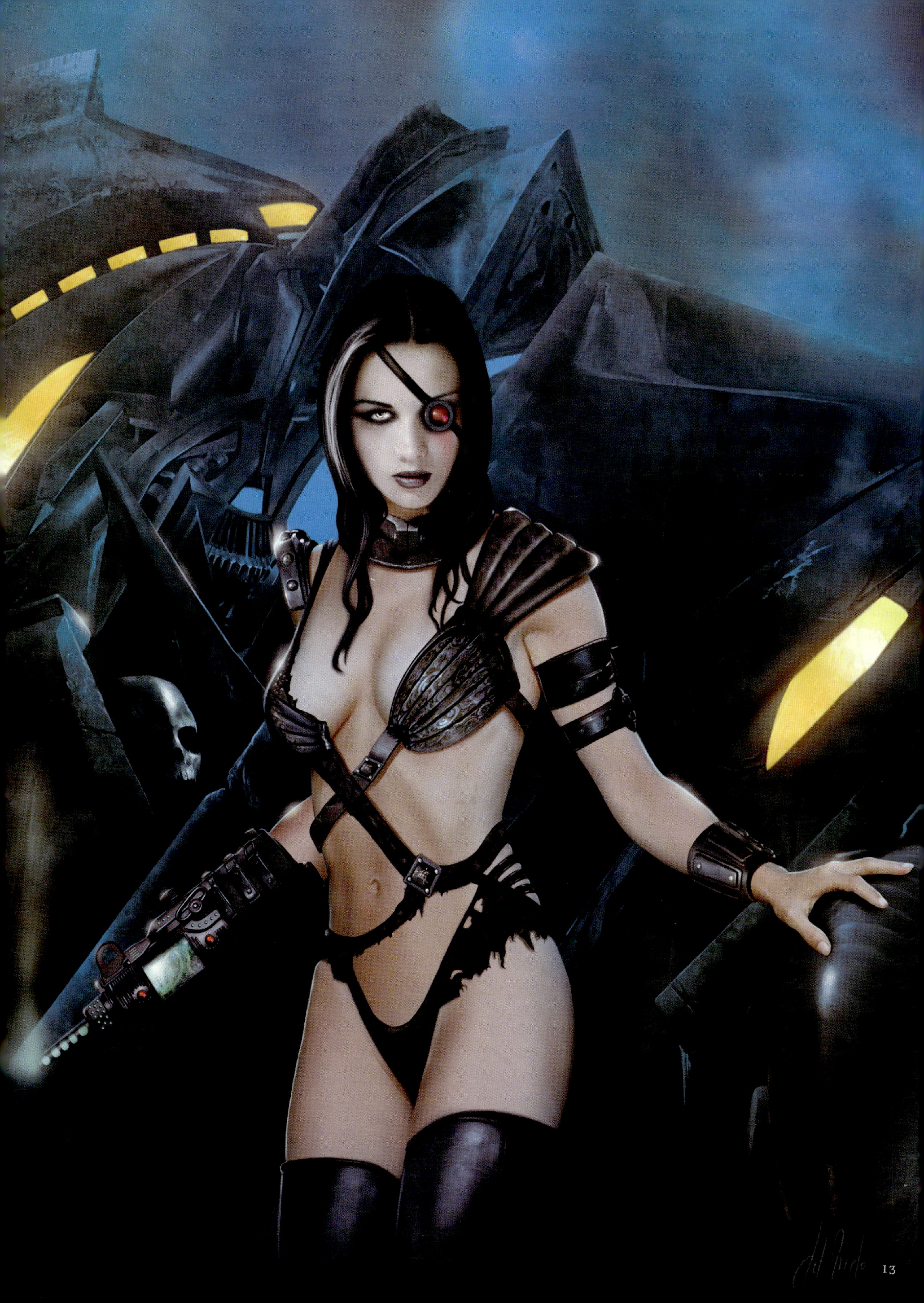

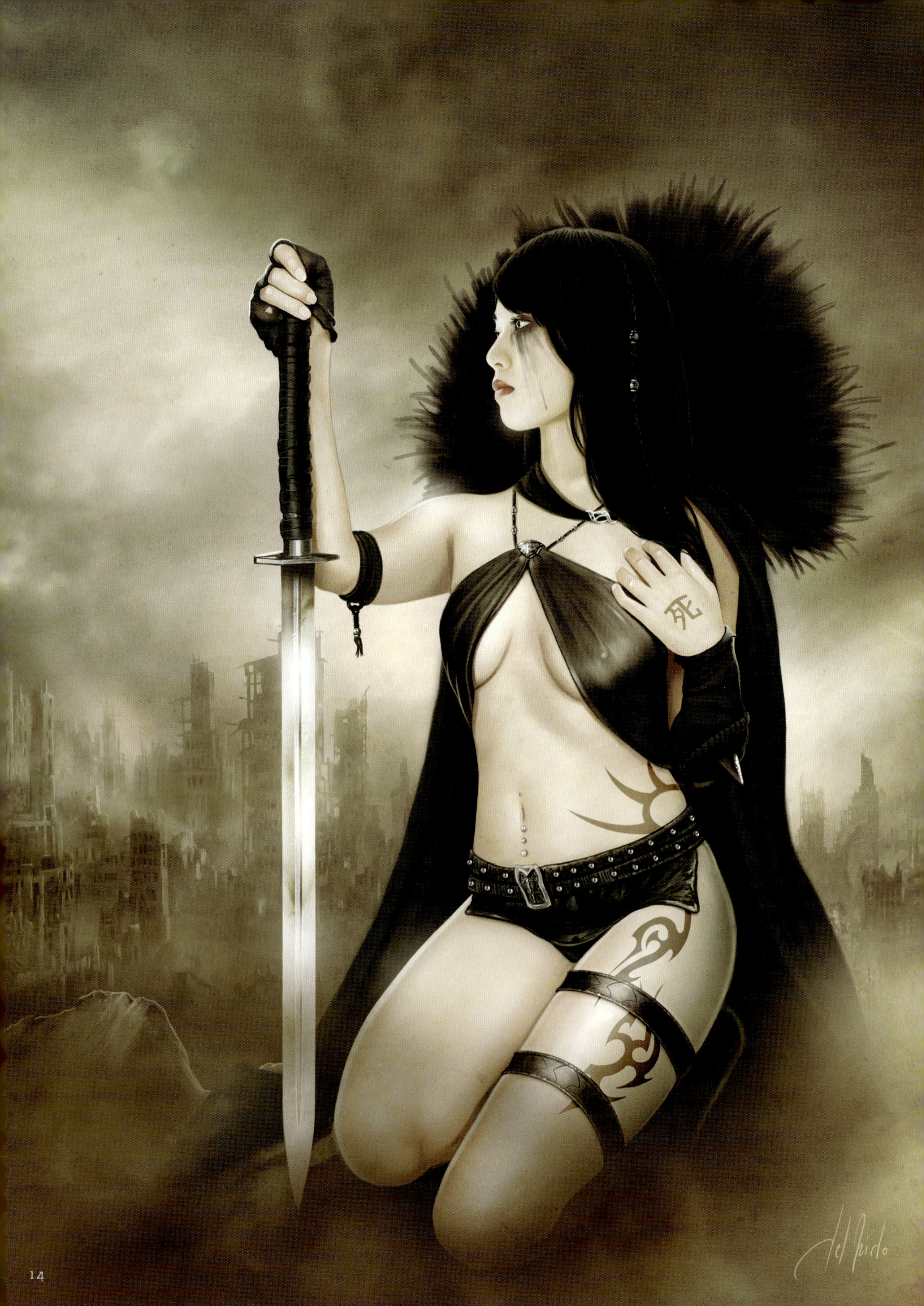
死

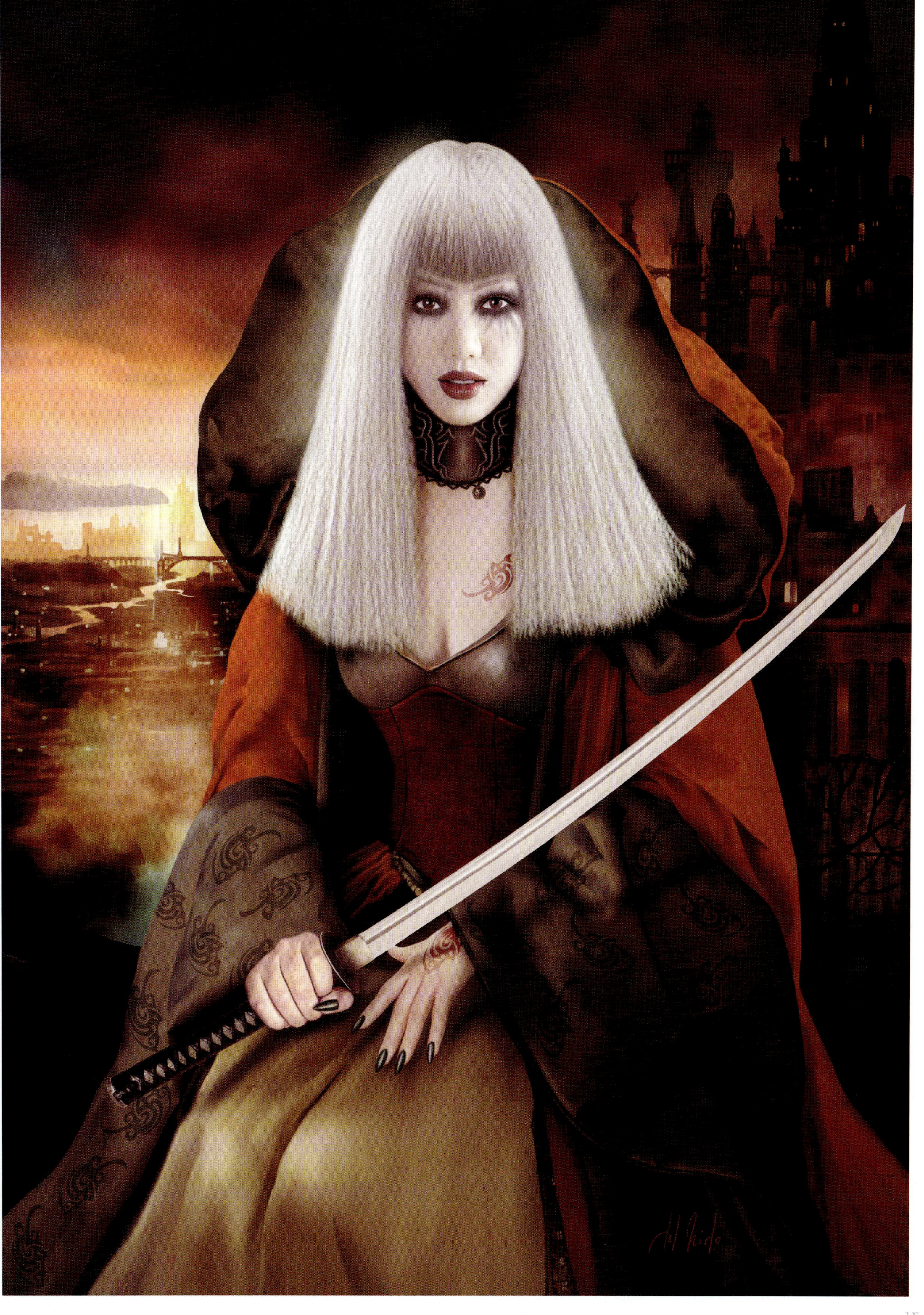

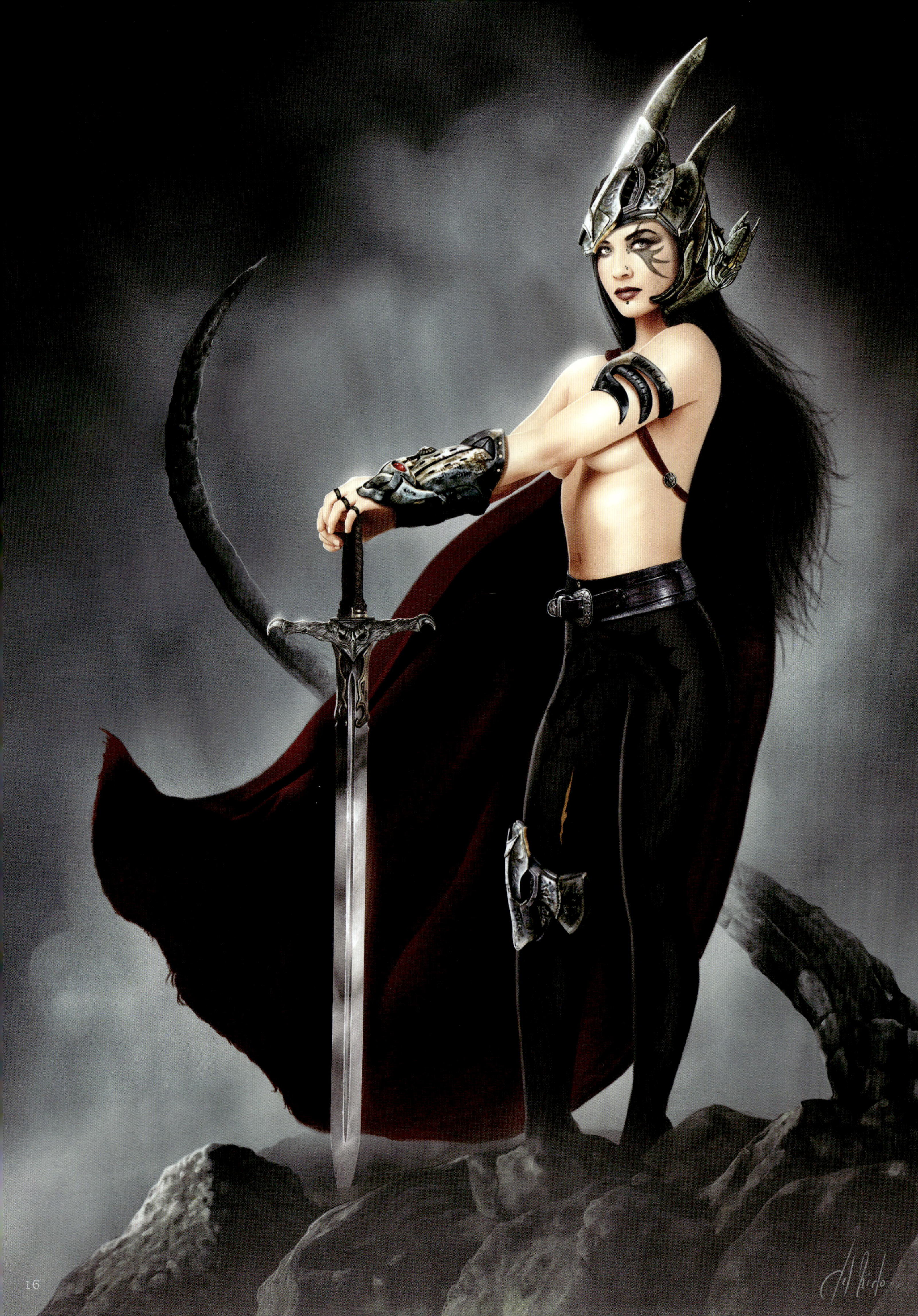

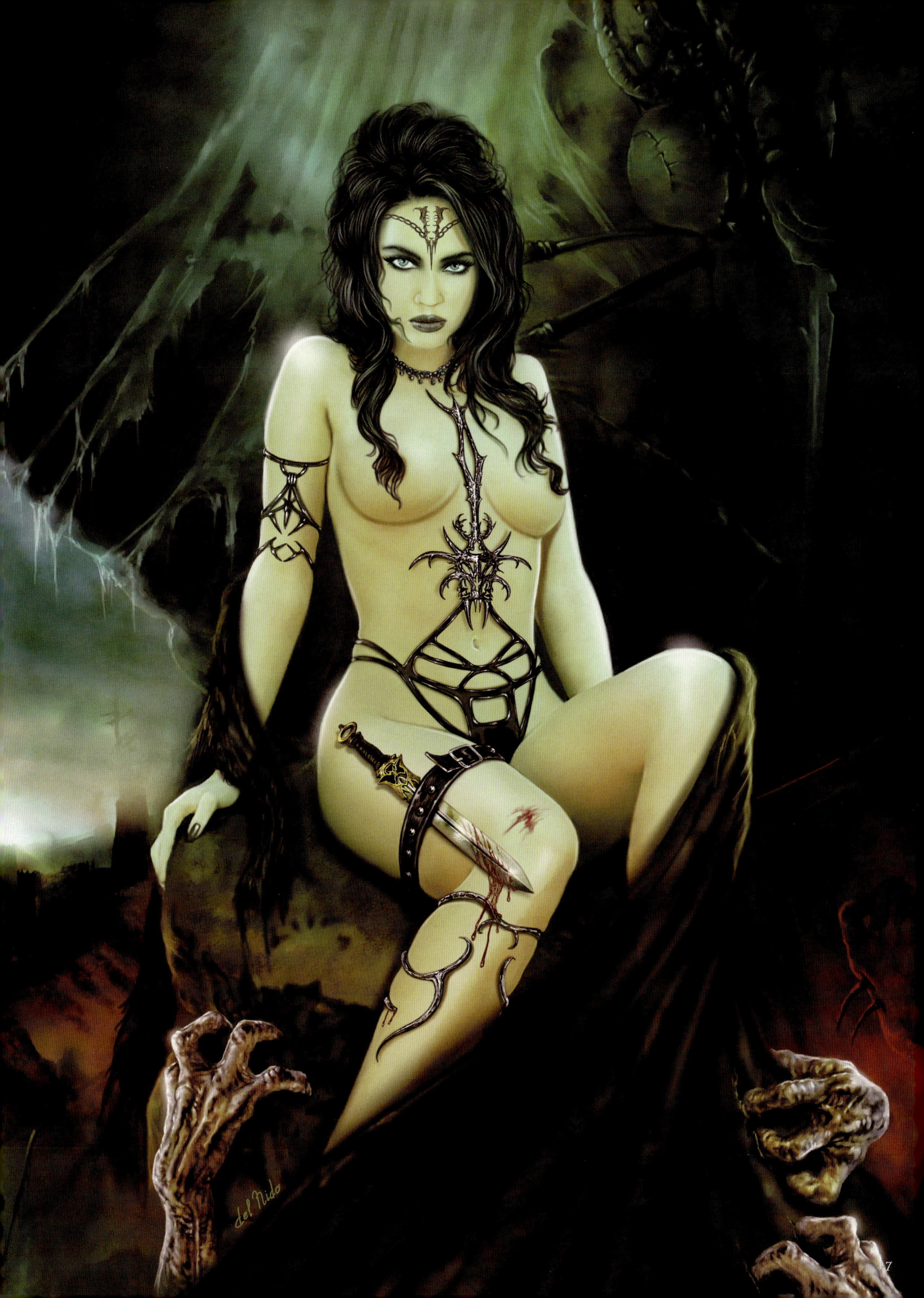
del Nido

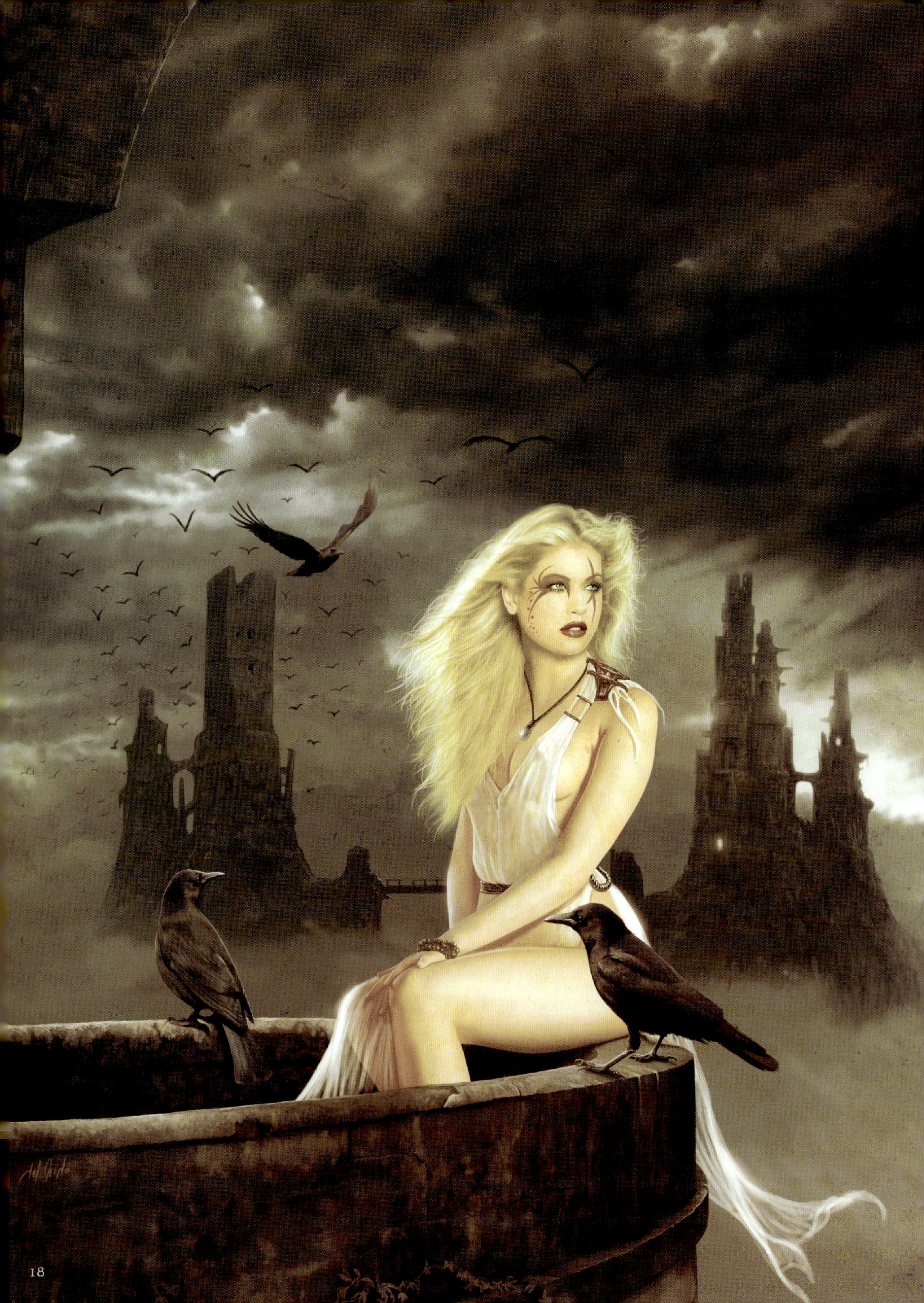

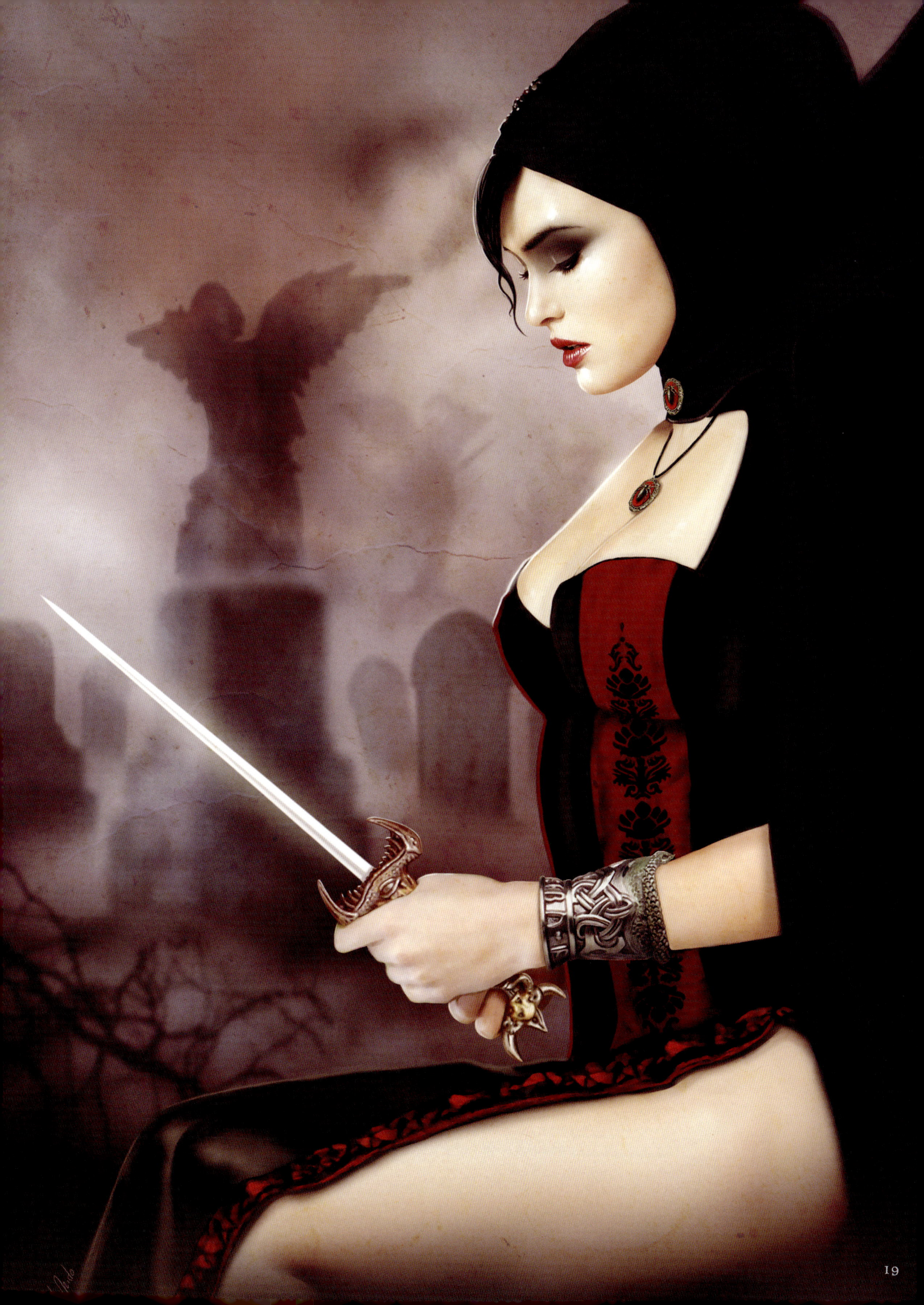

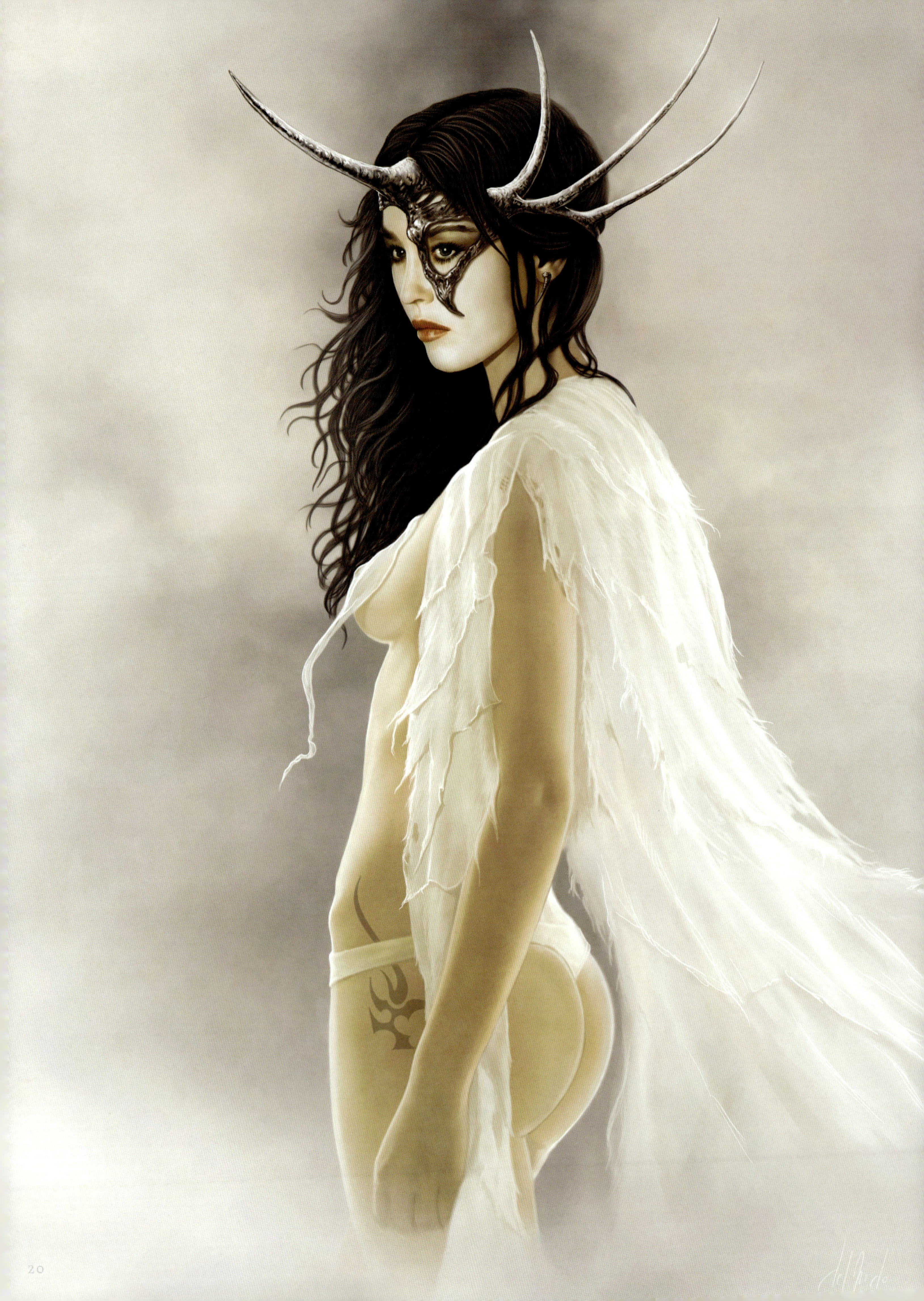

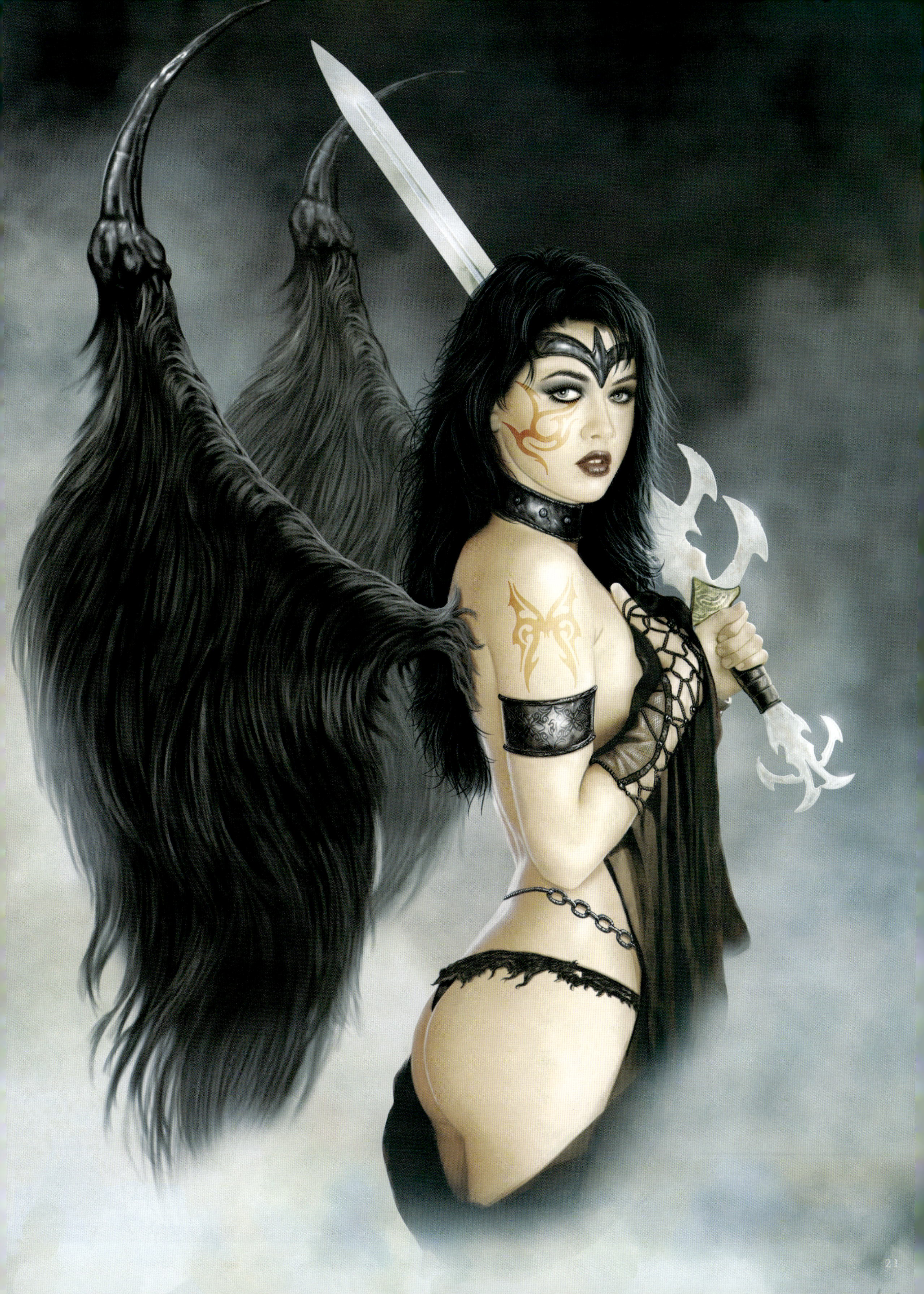

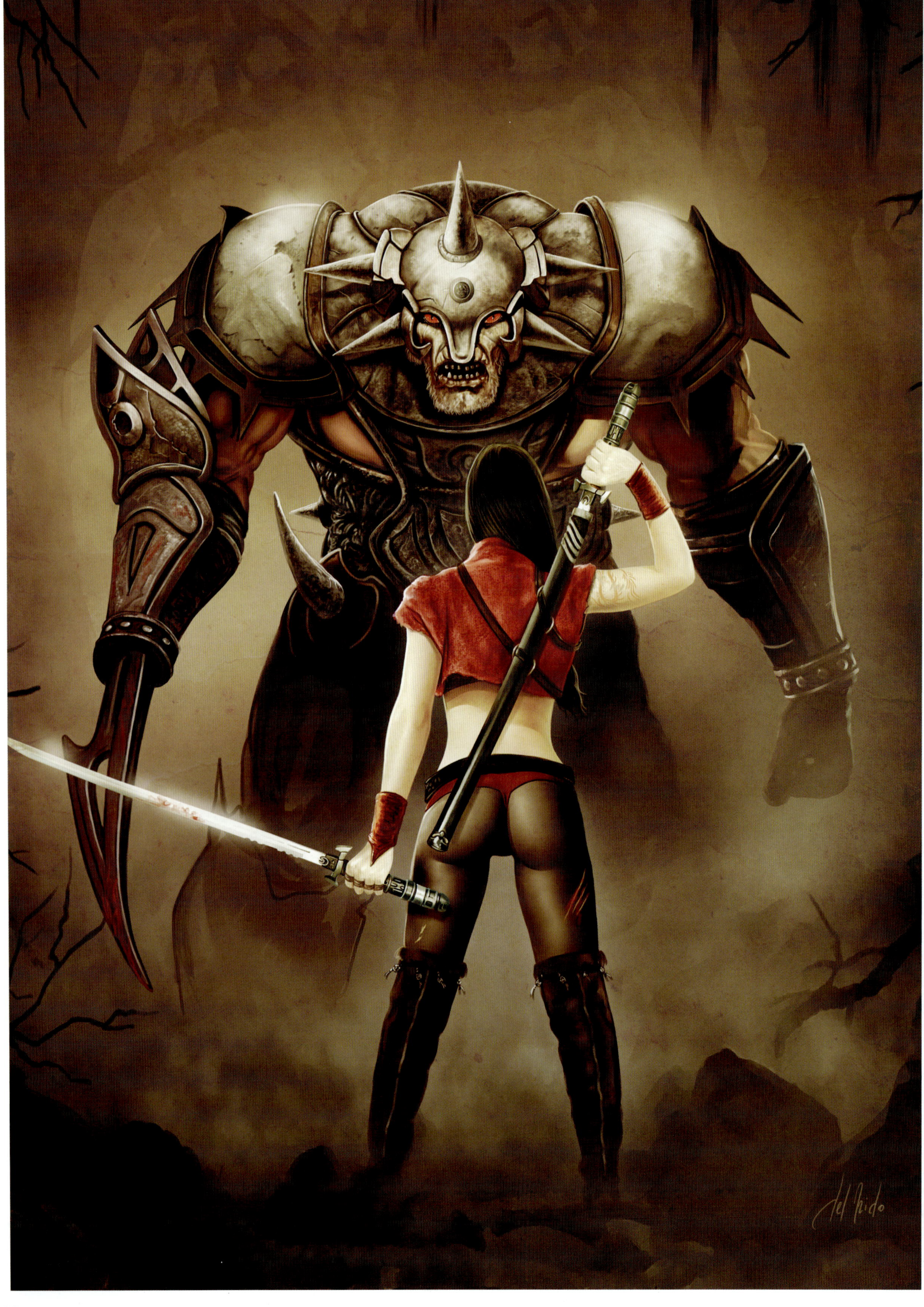

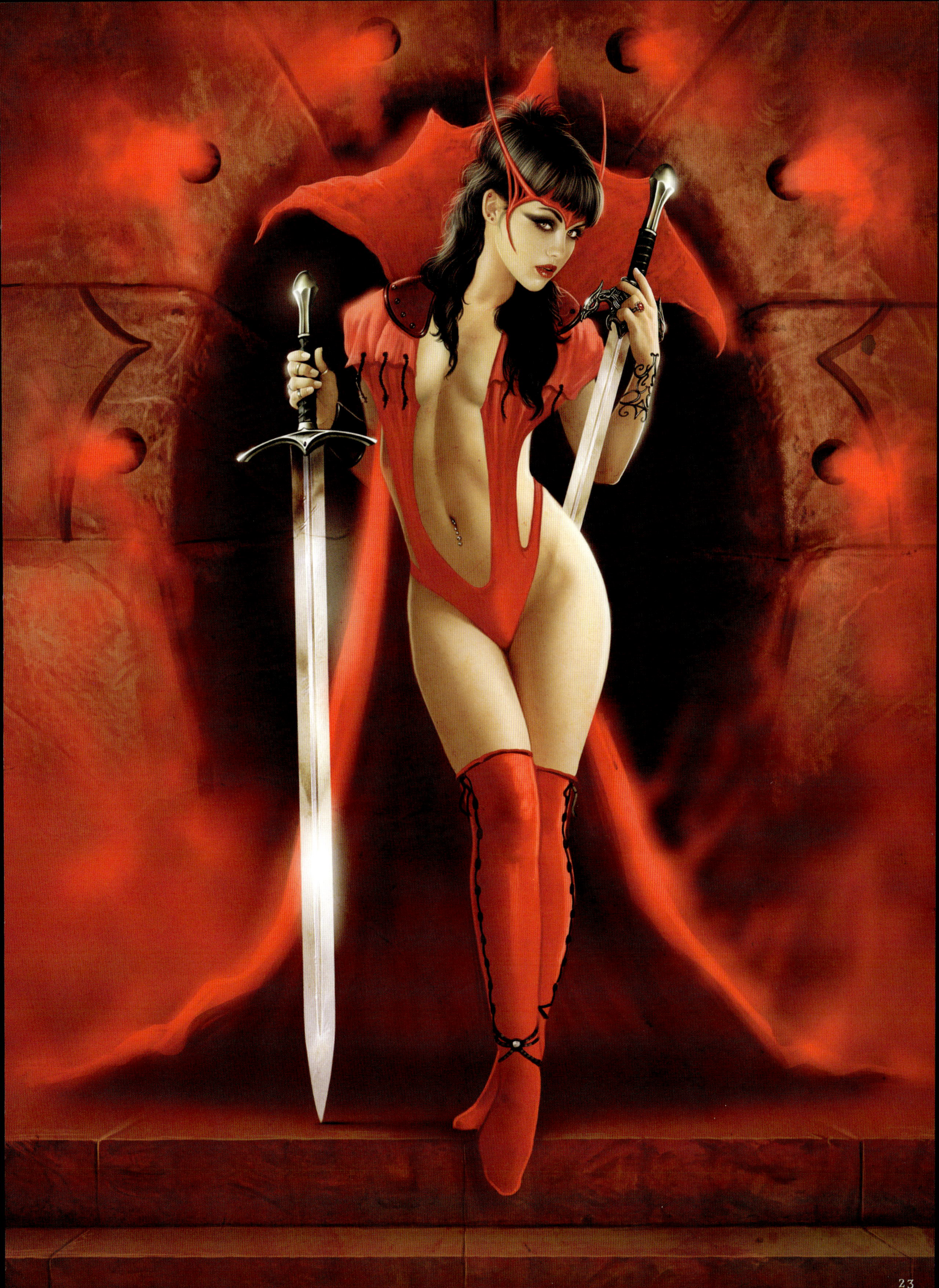

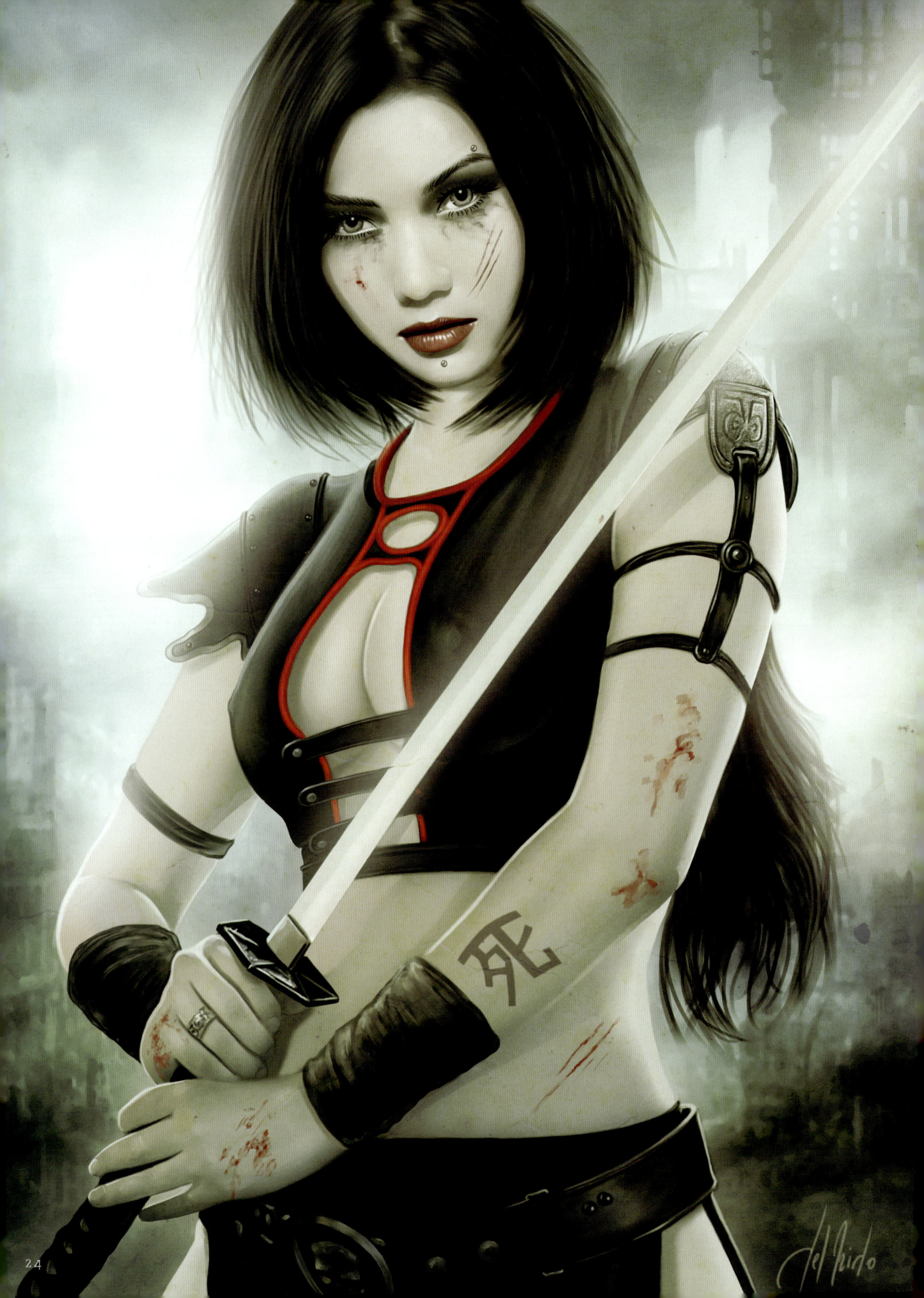

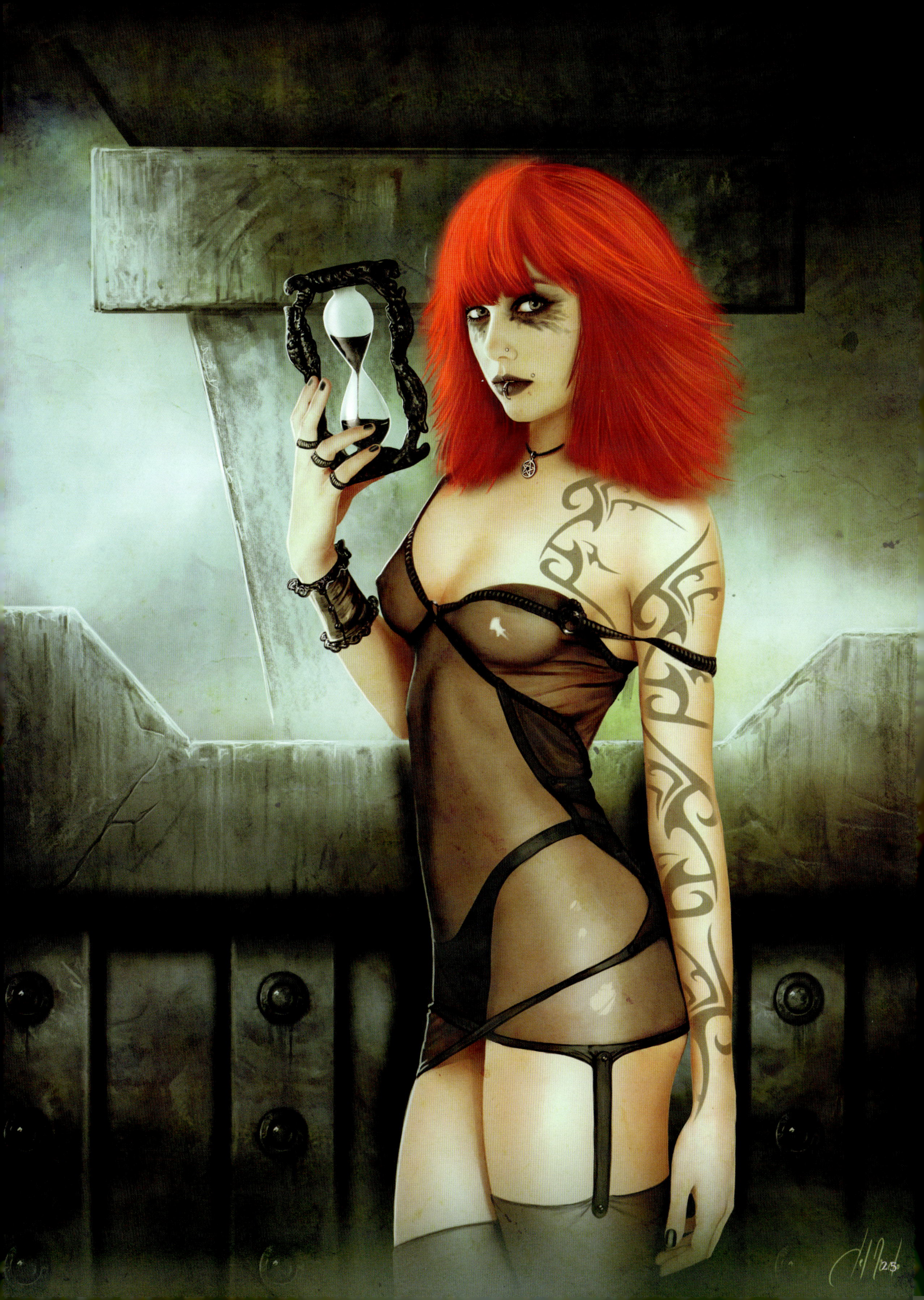

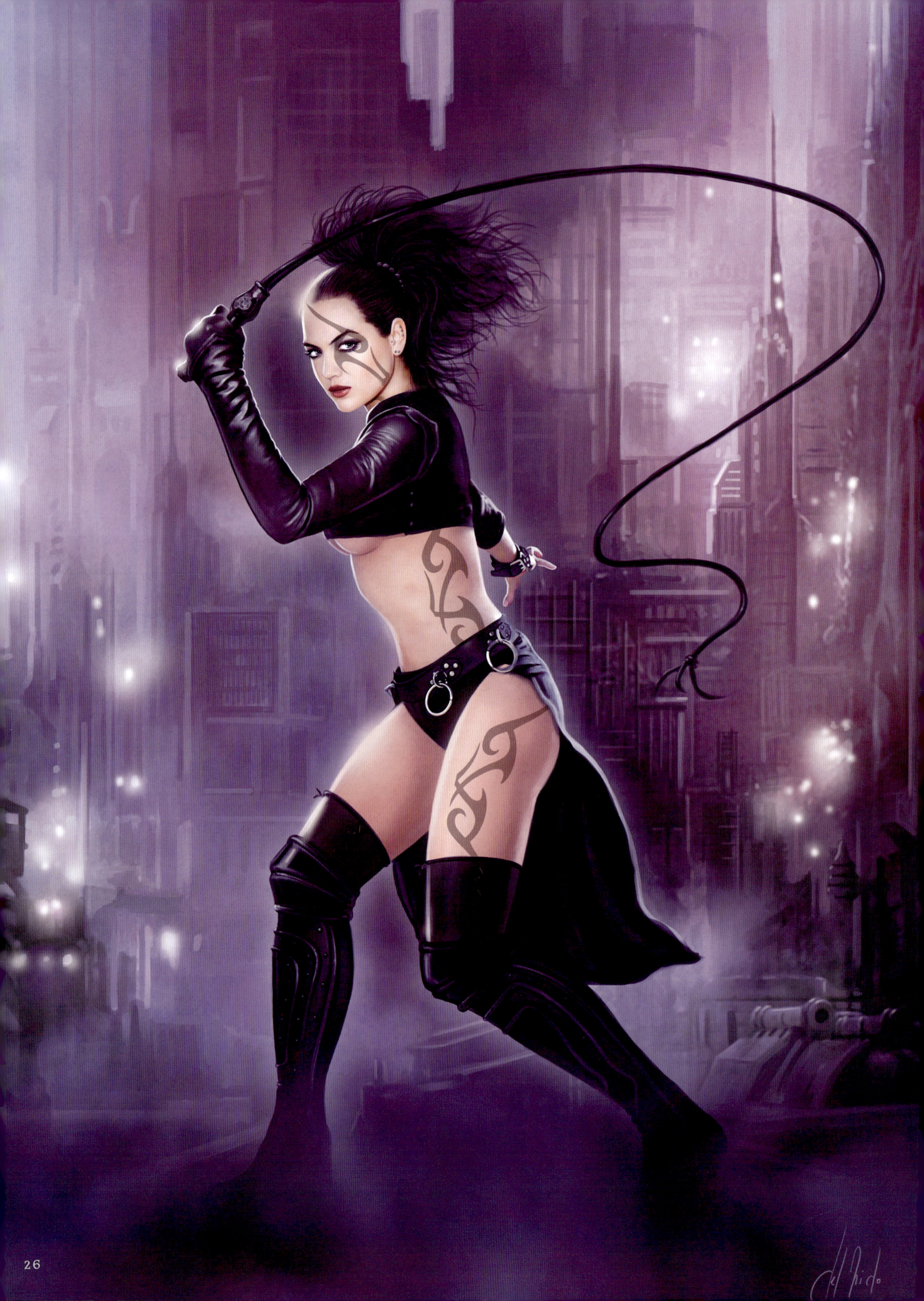

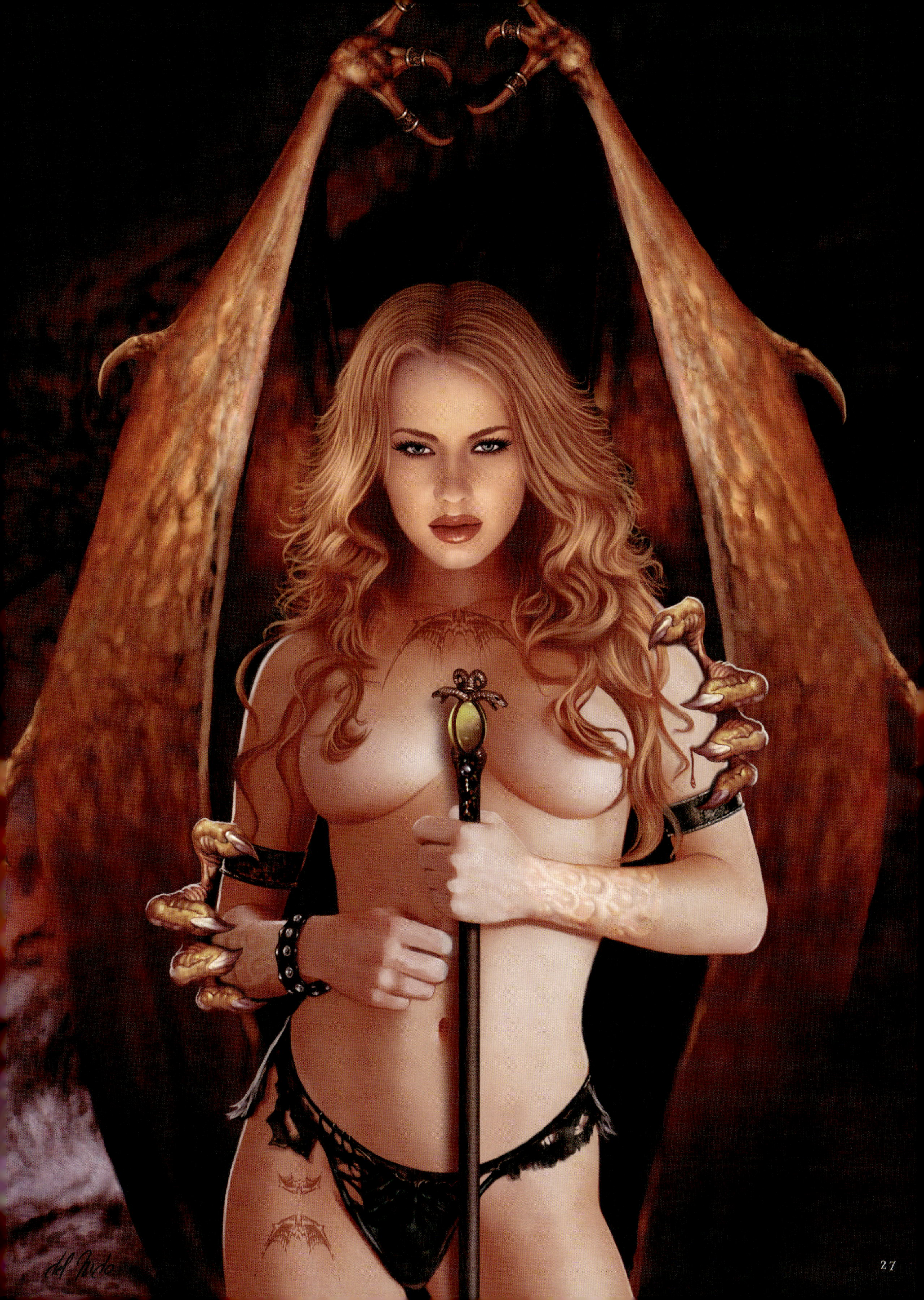

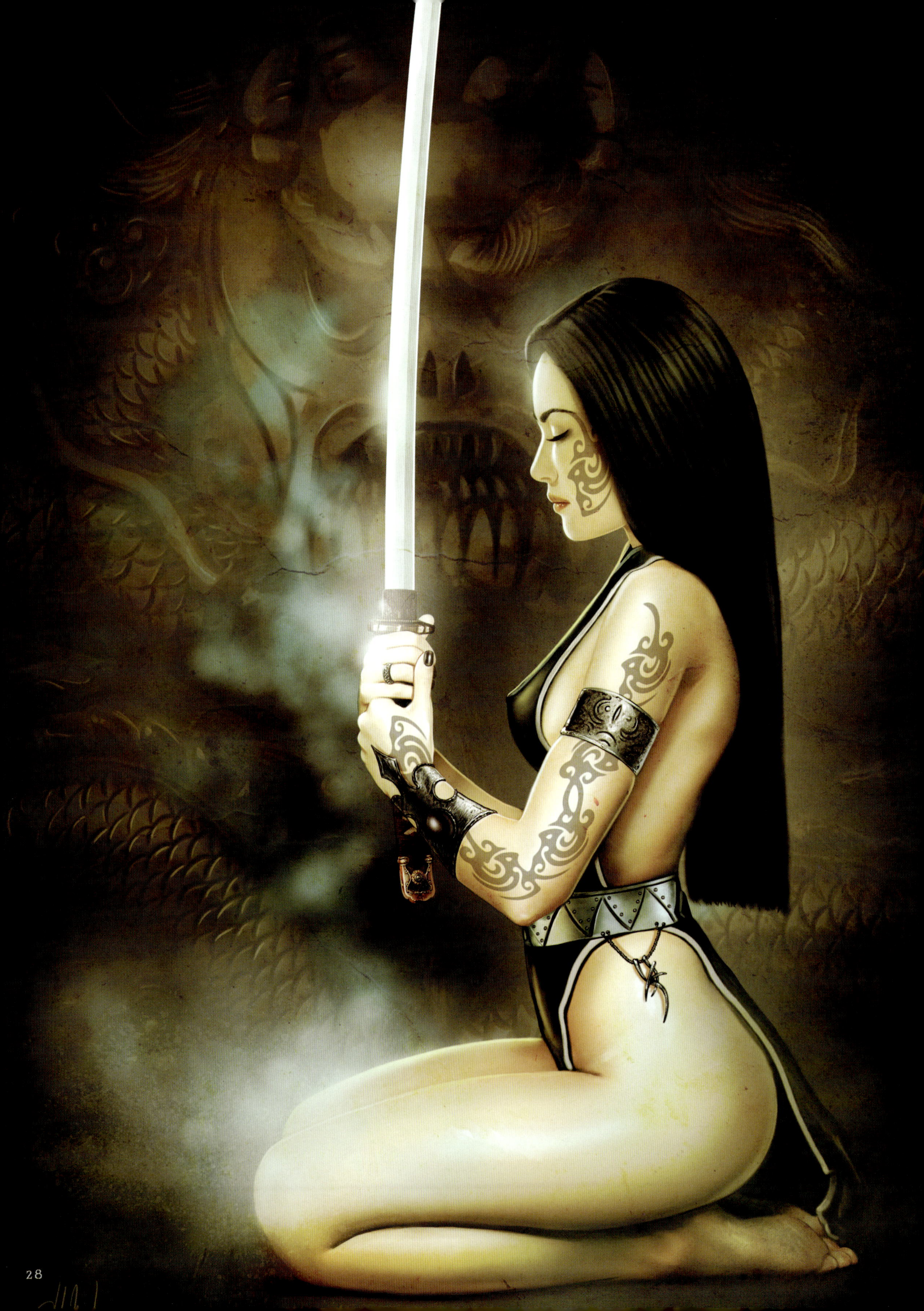

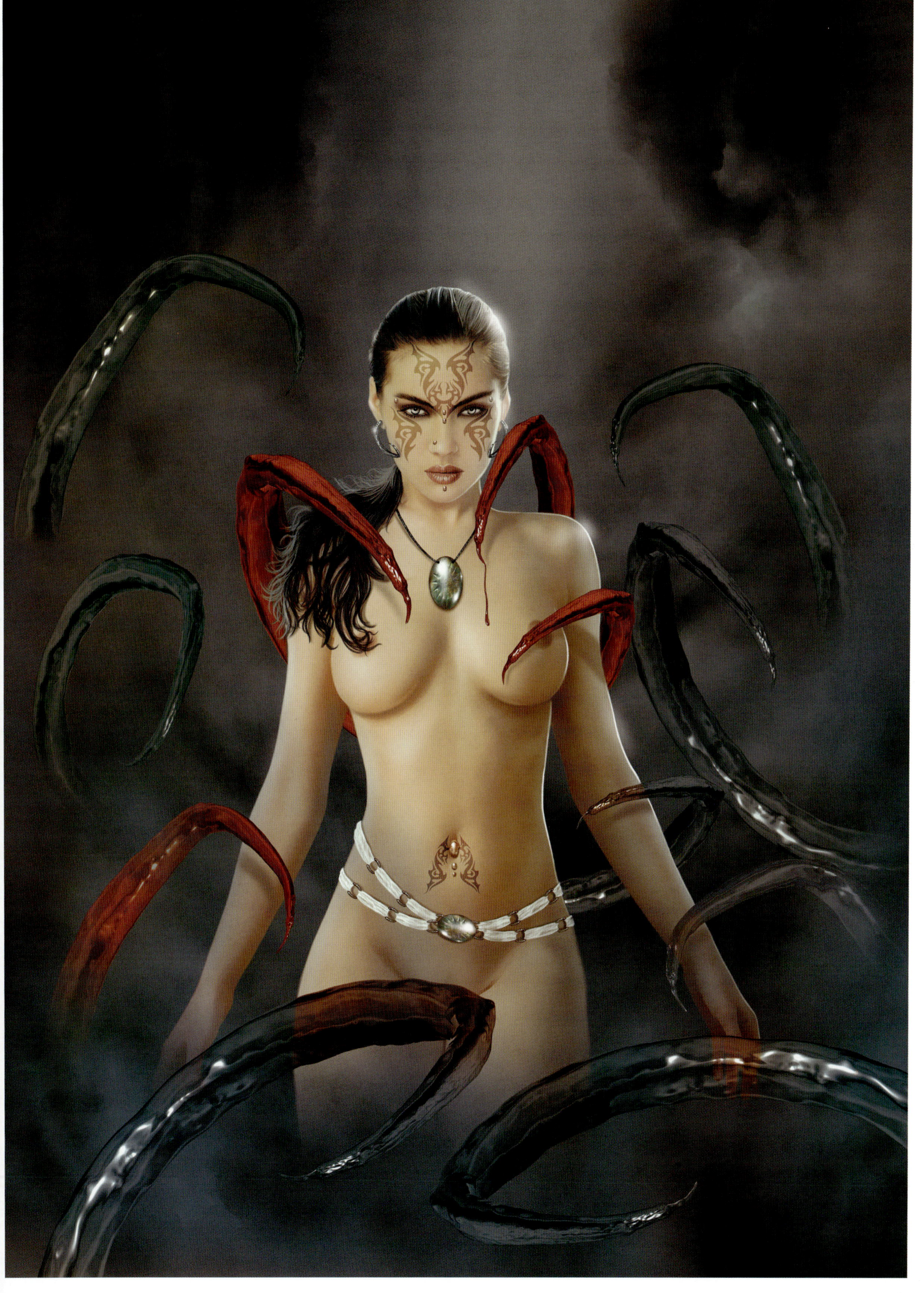

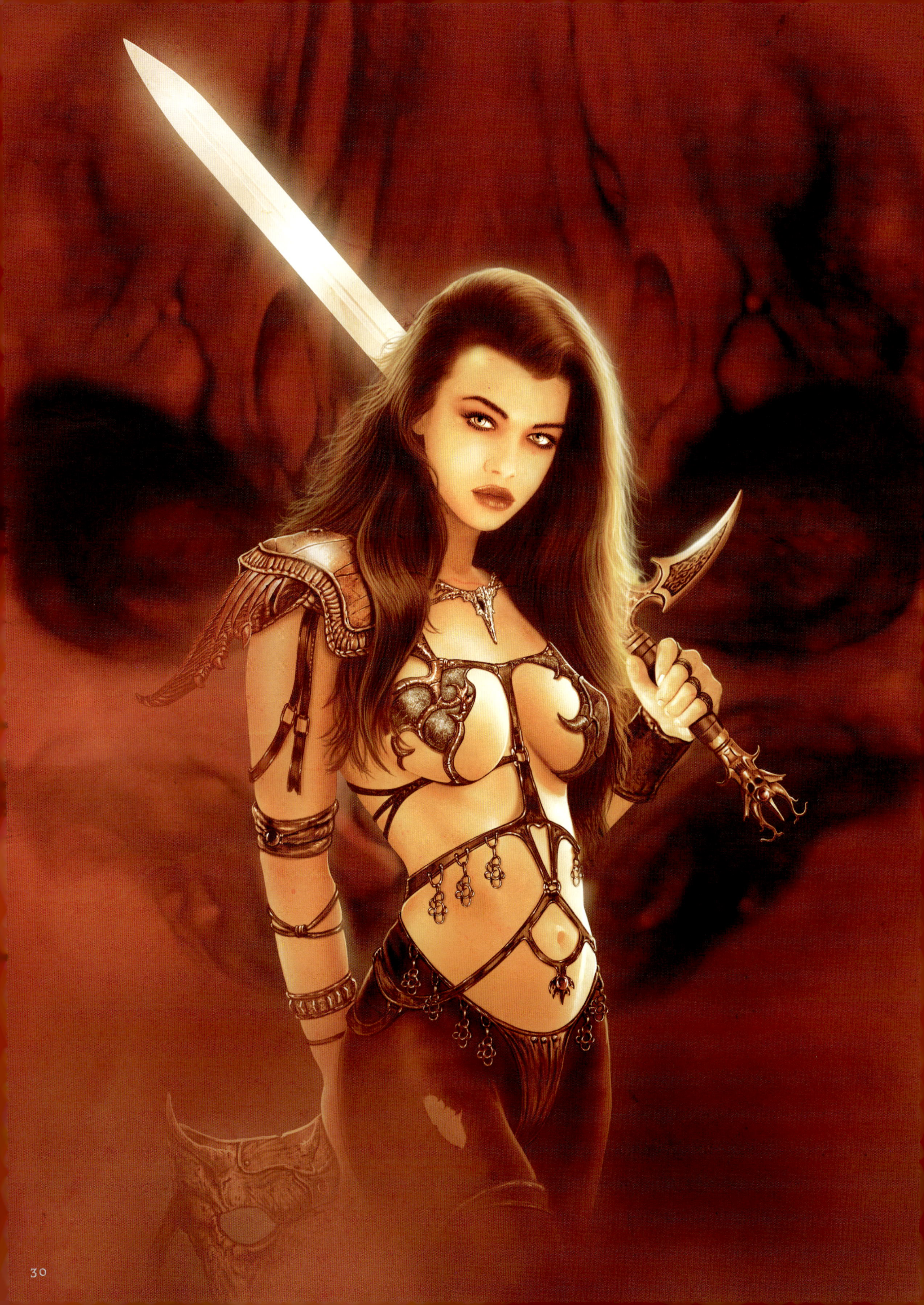

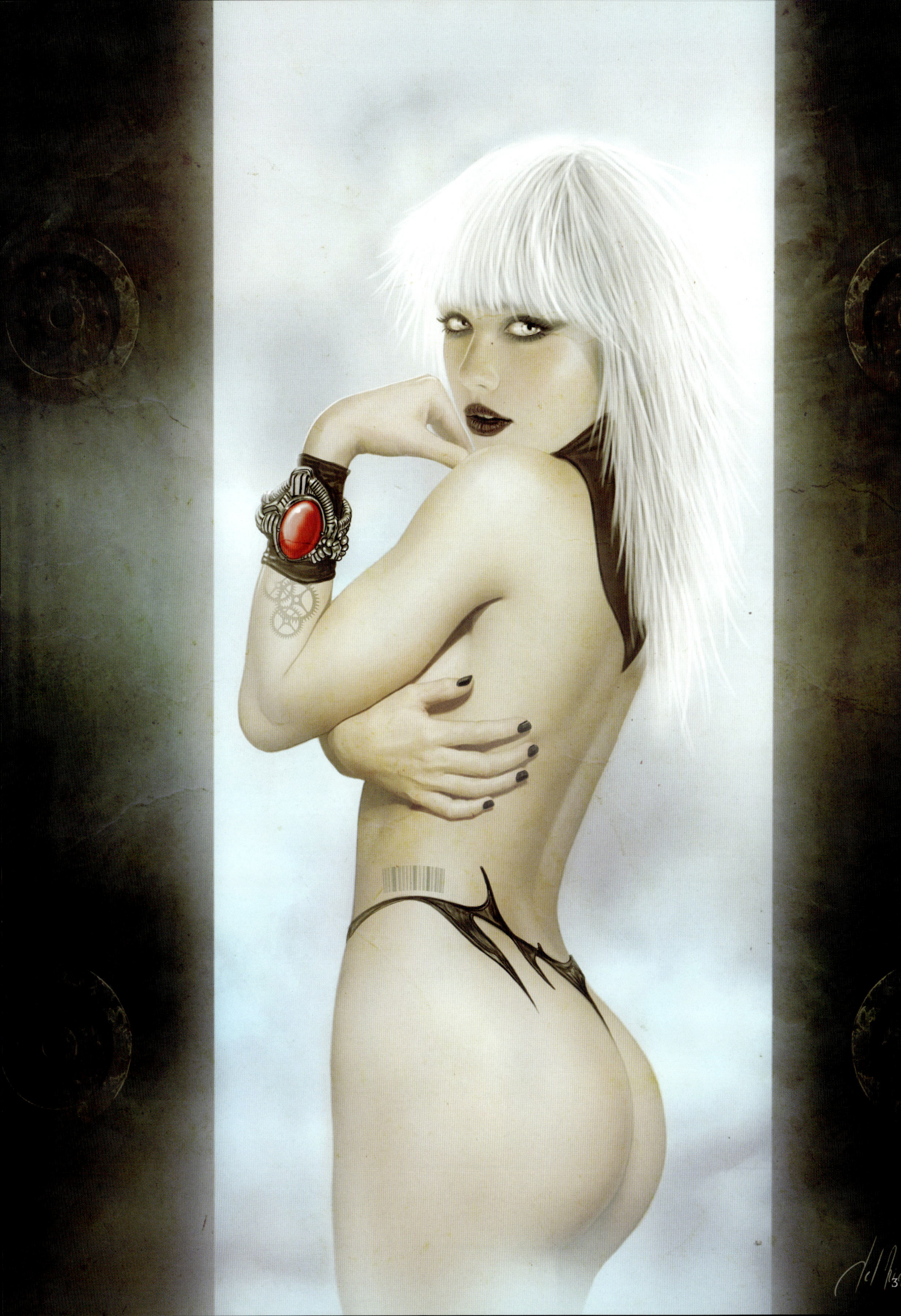

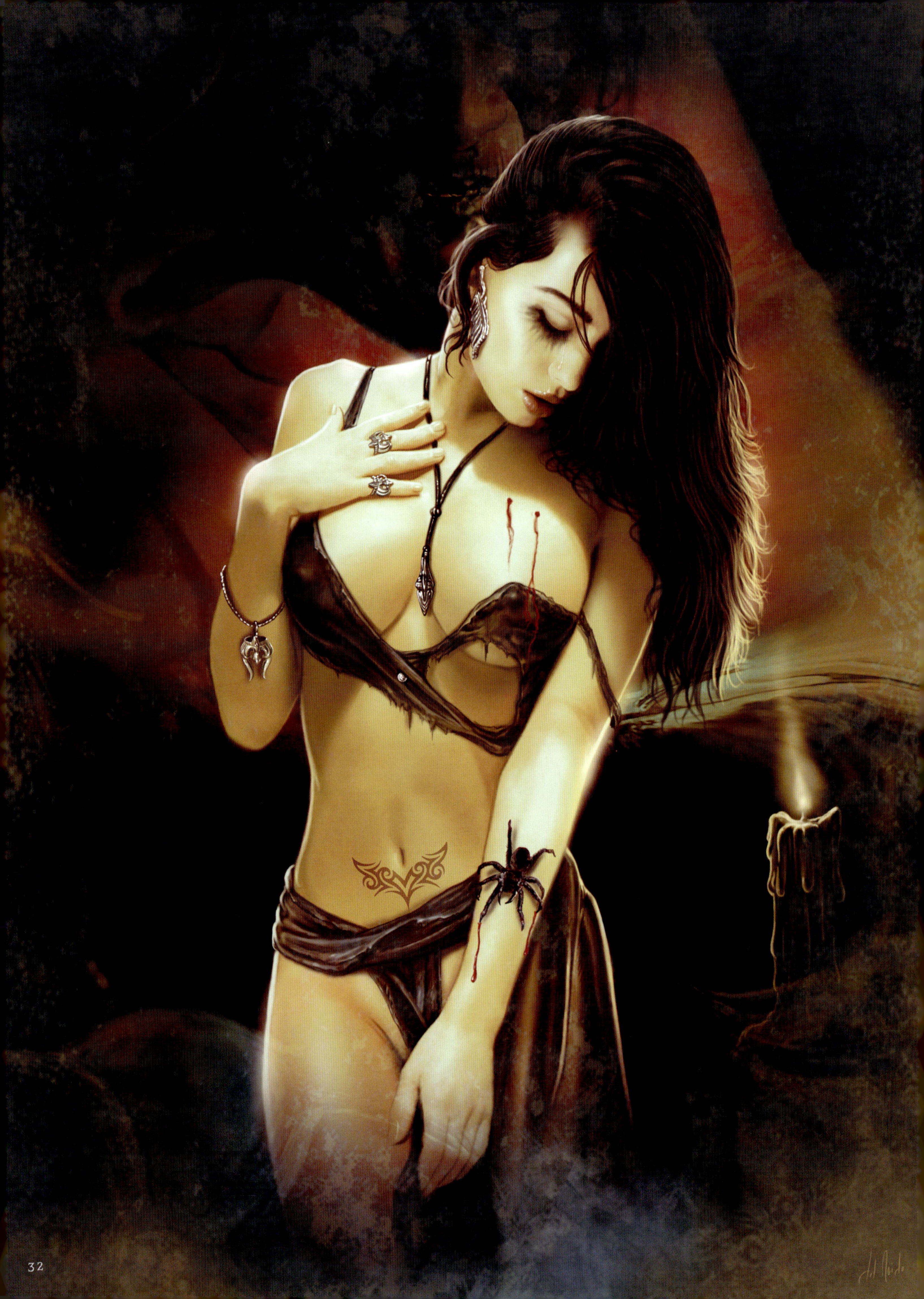

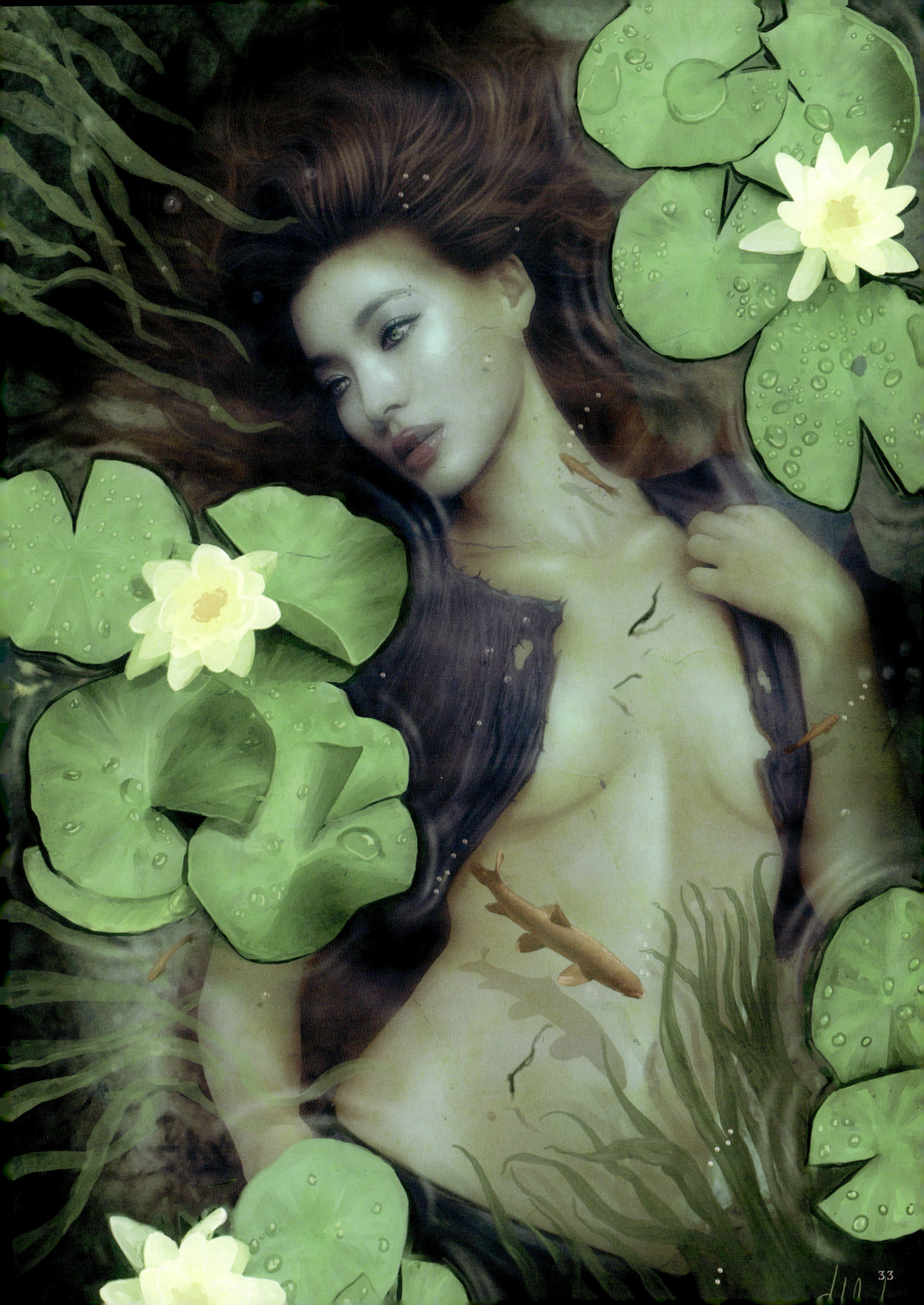

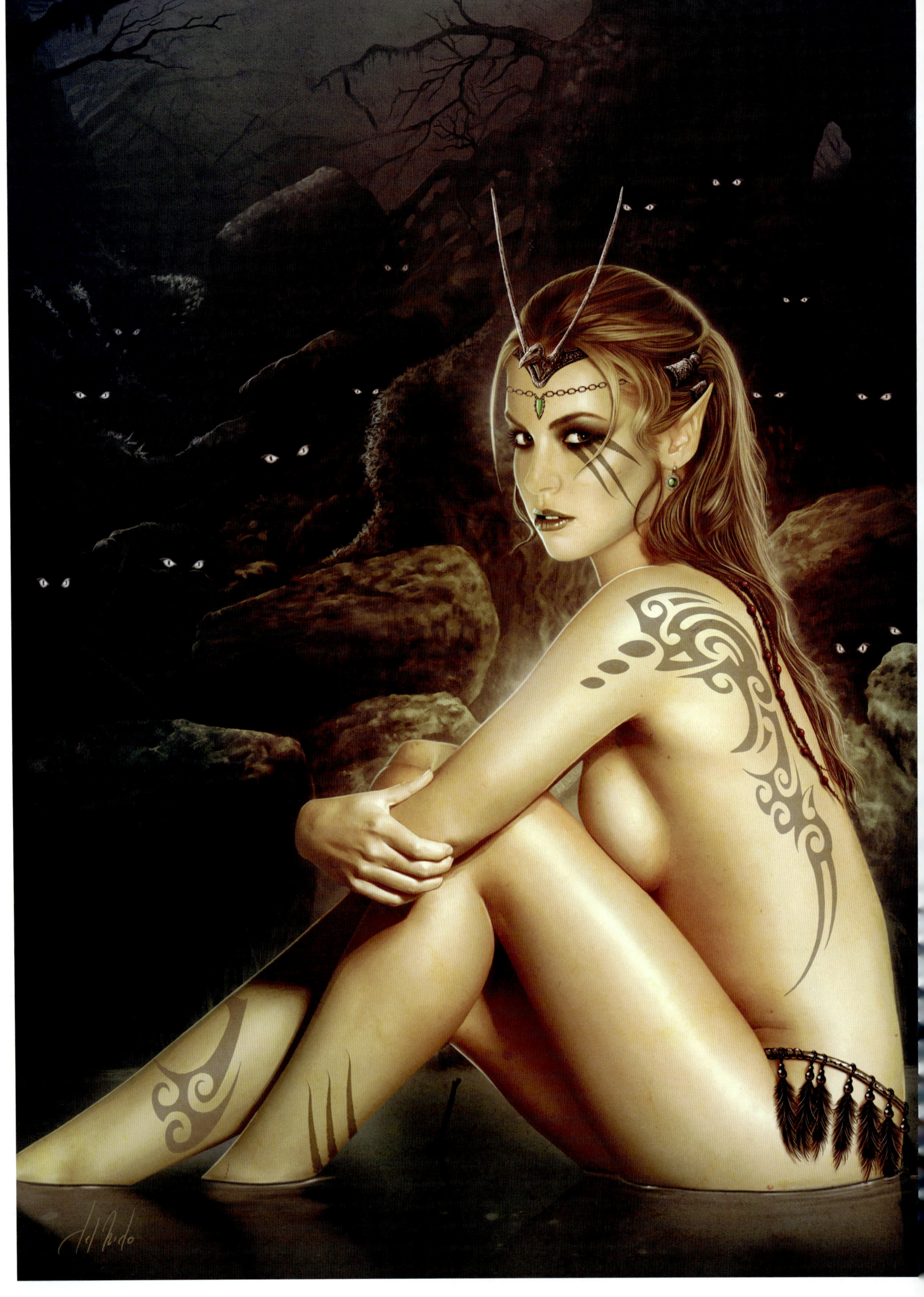

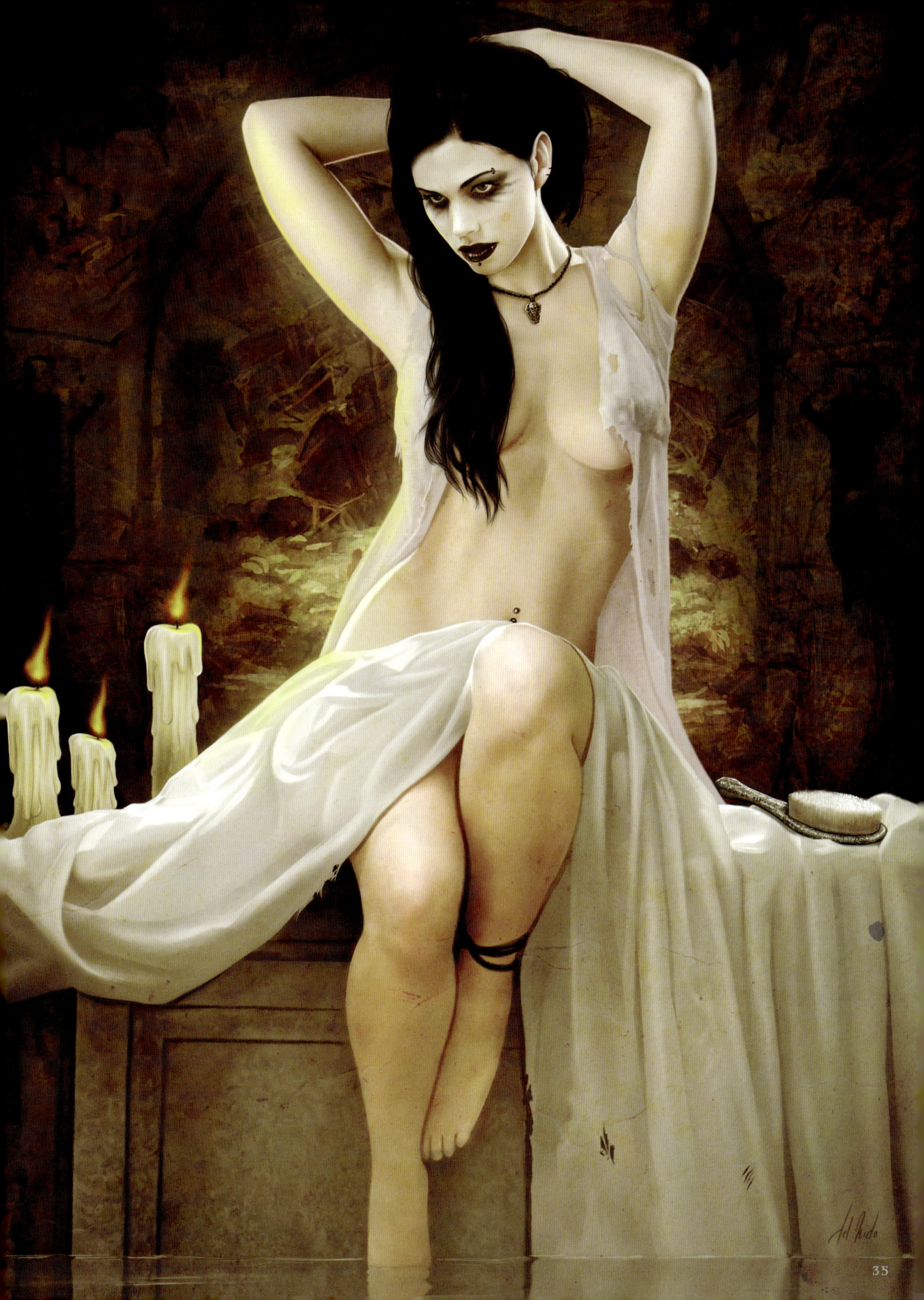

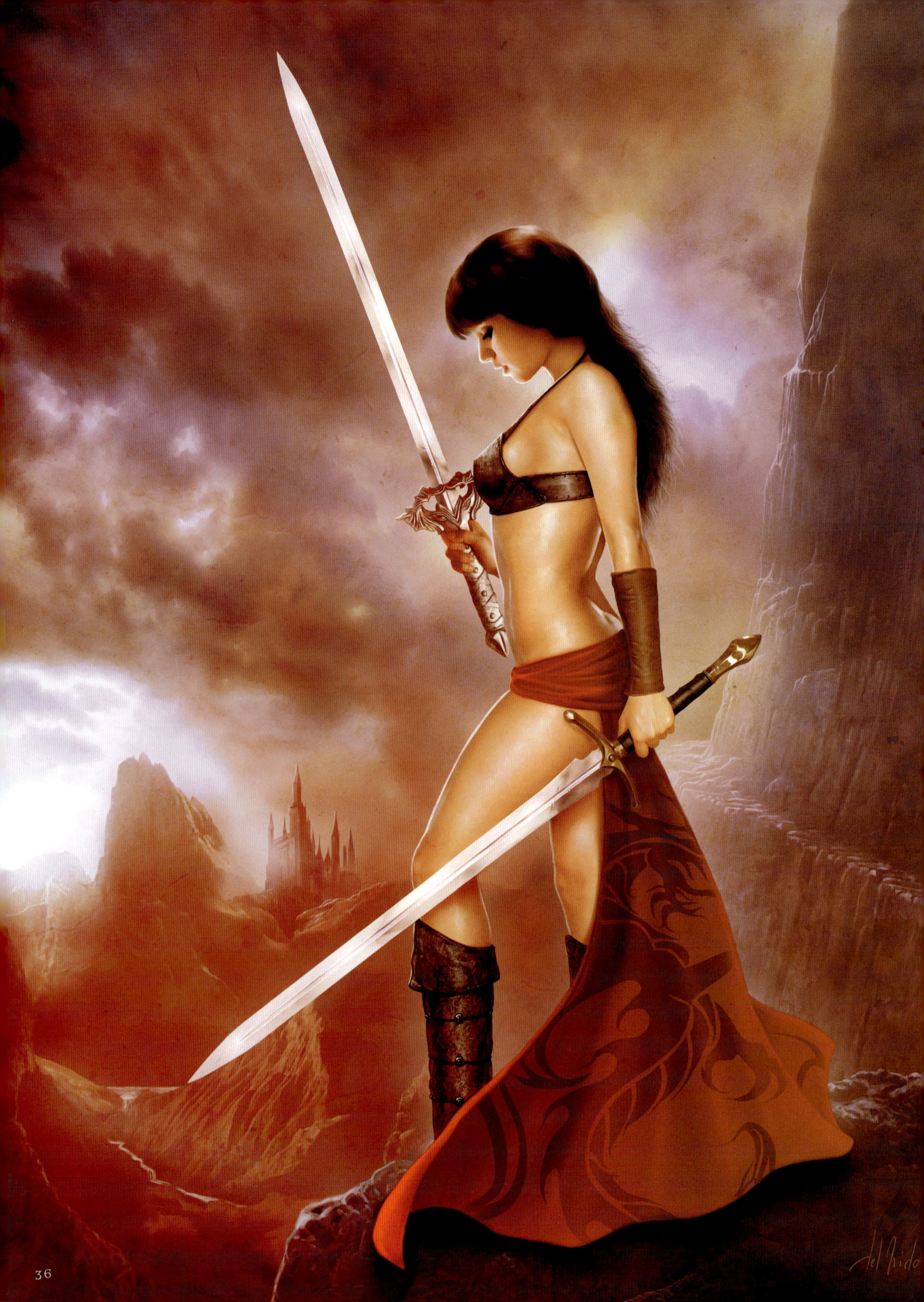

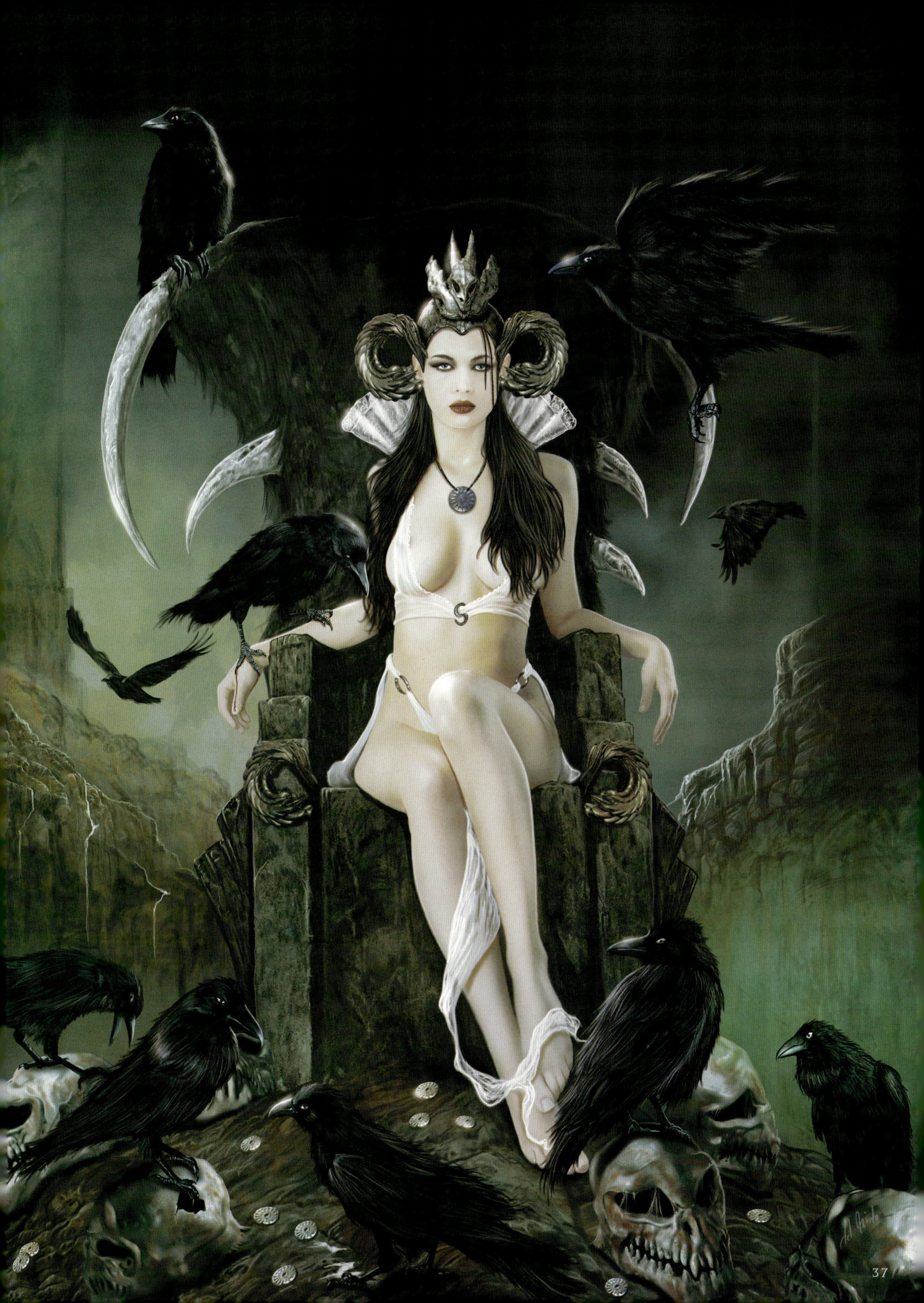

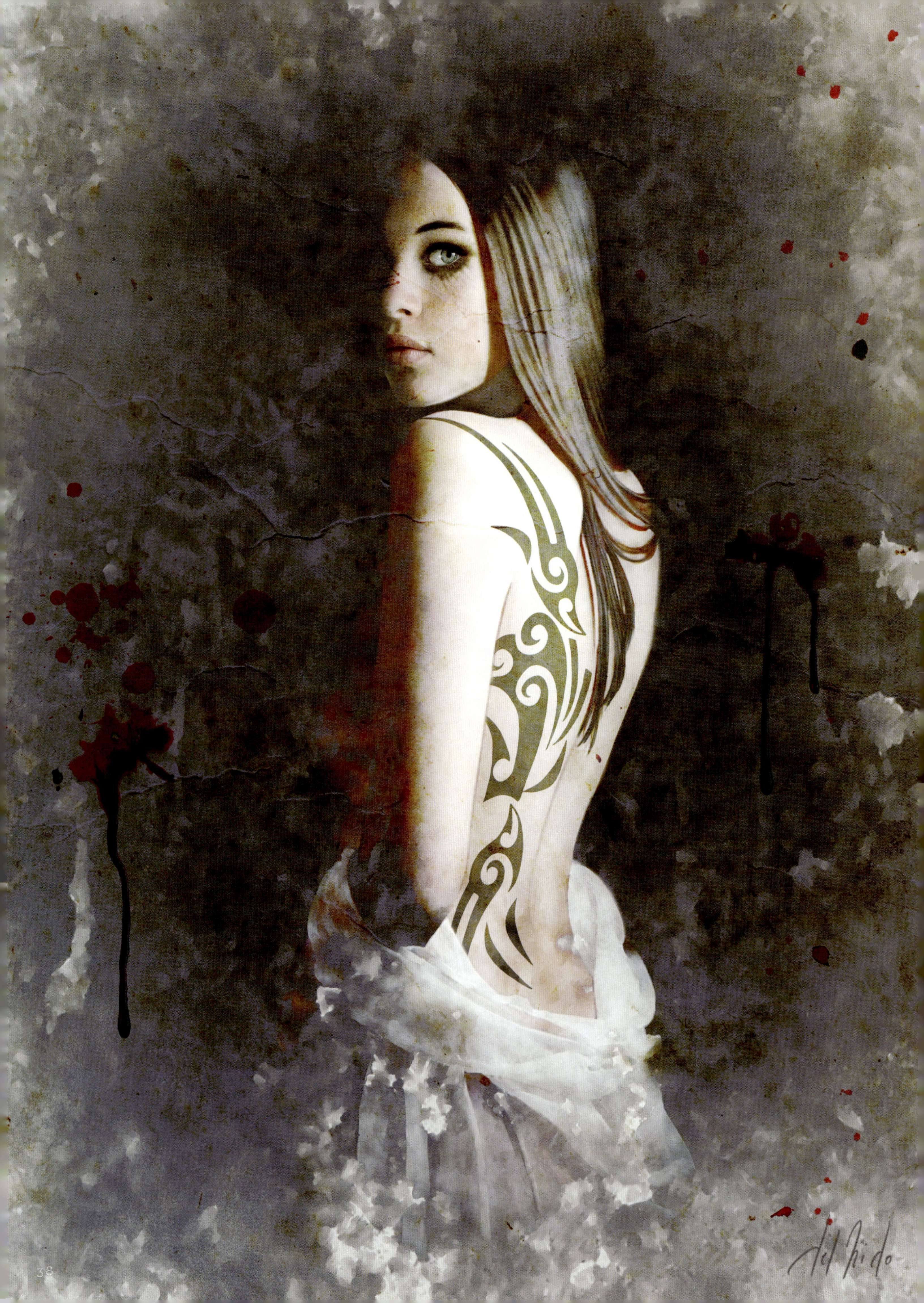

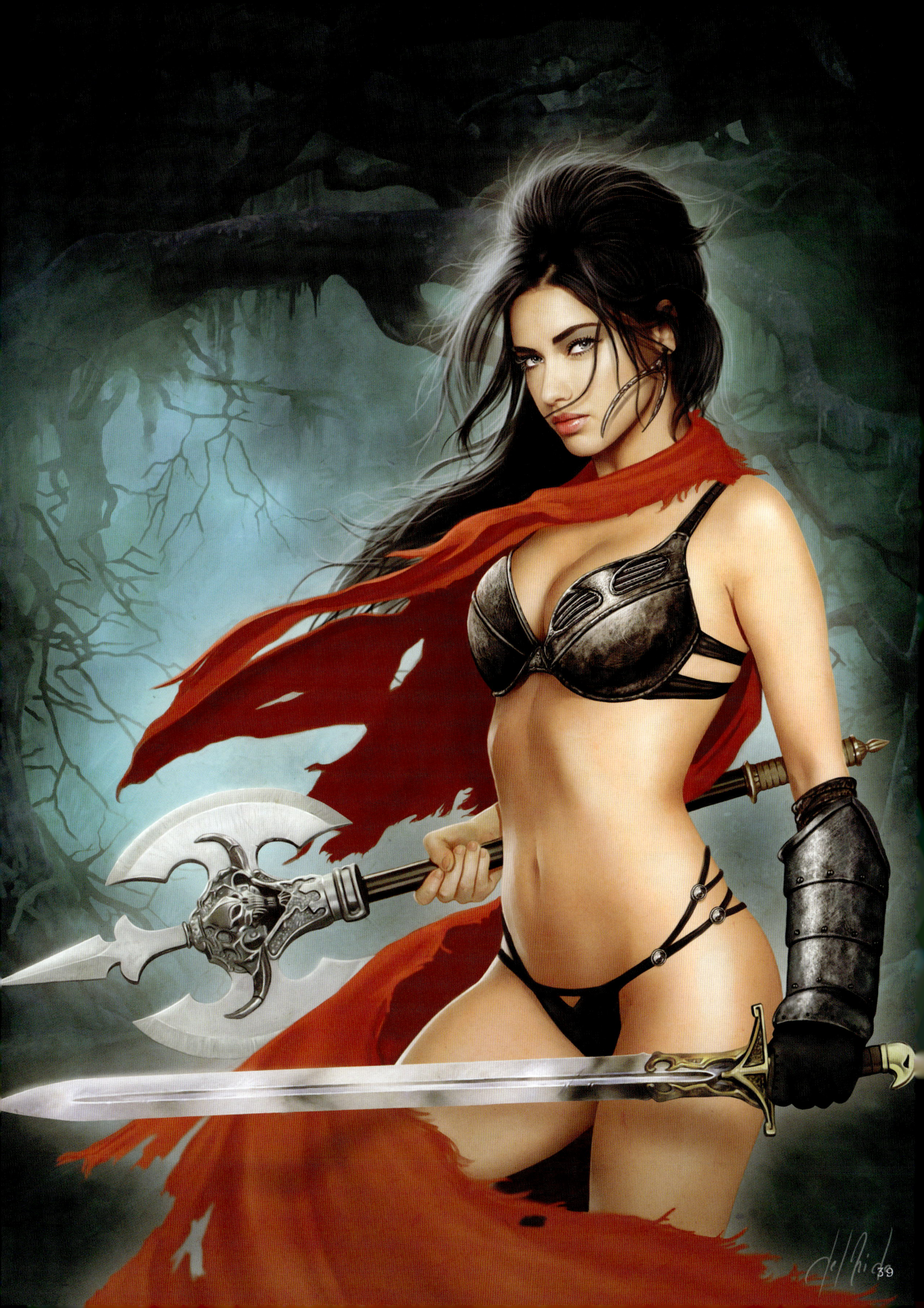

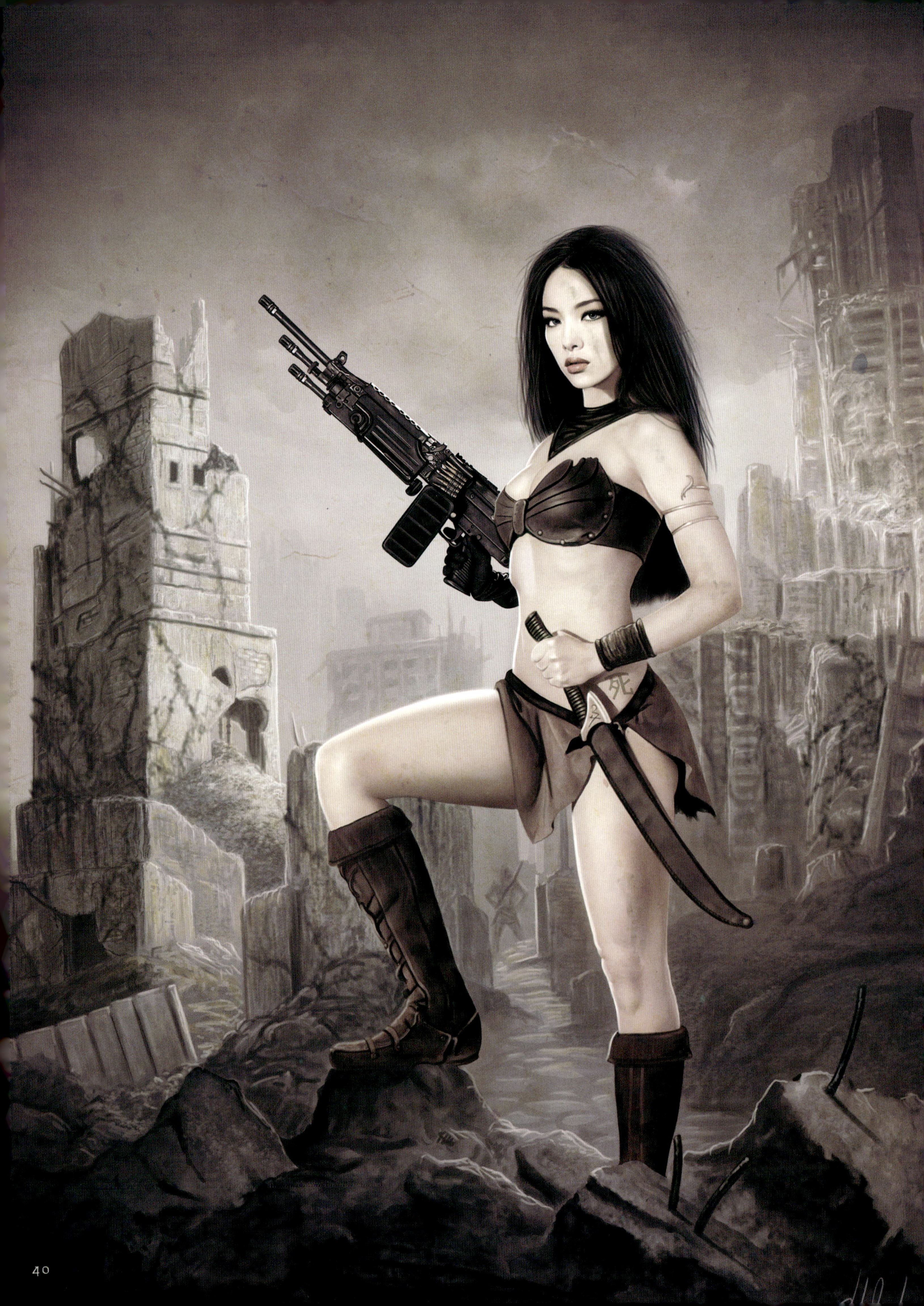
死

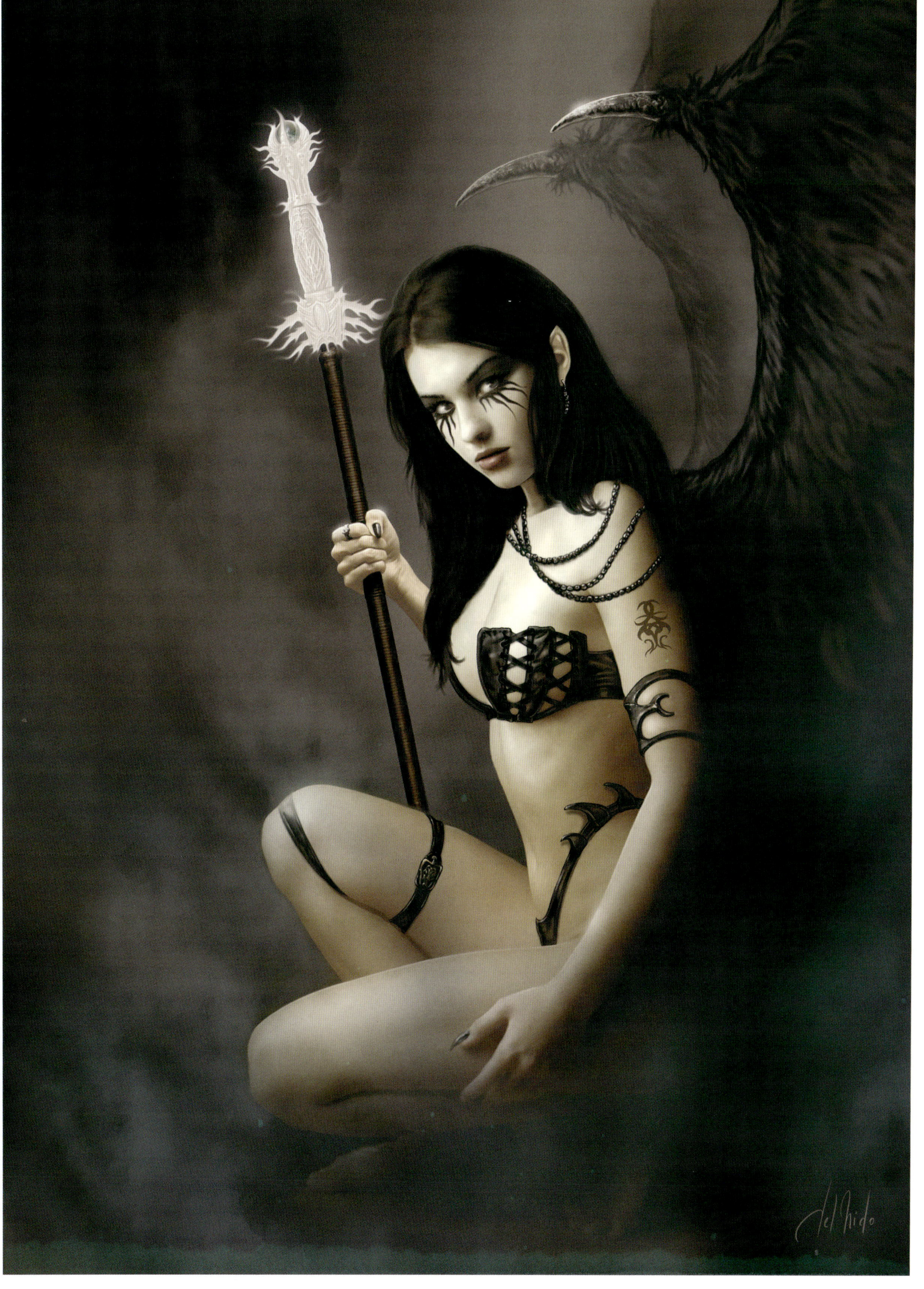
del Nido

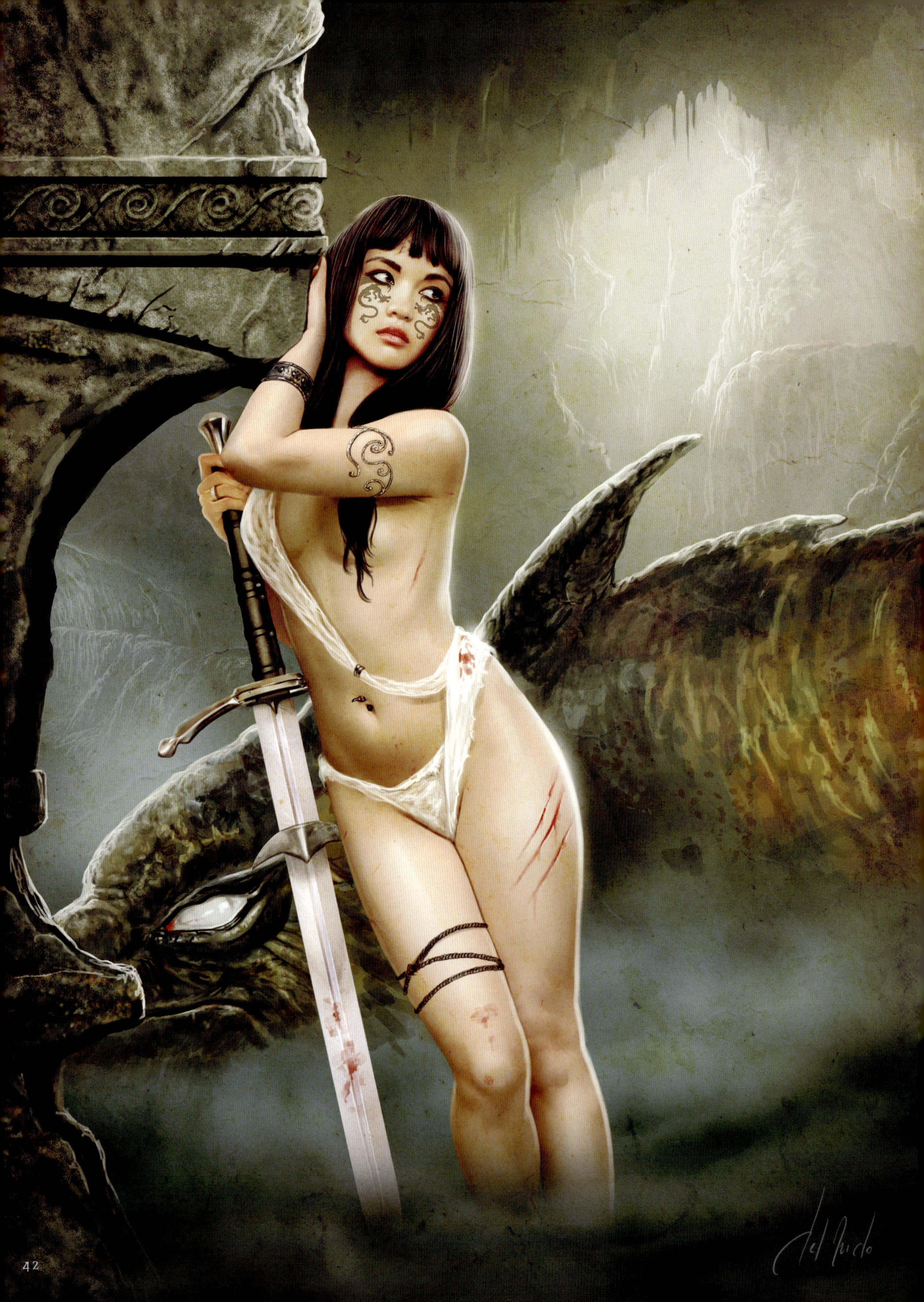

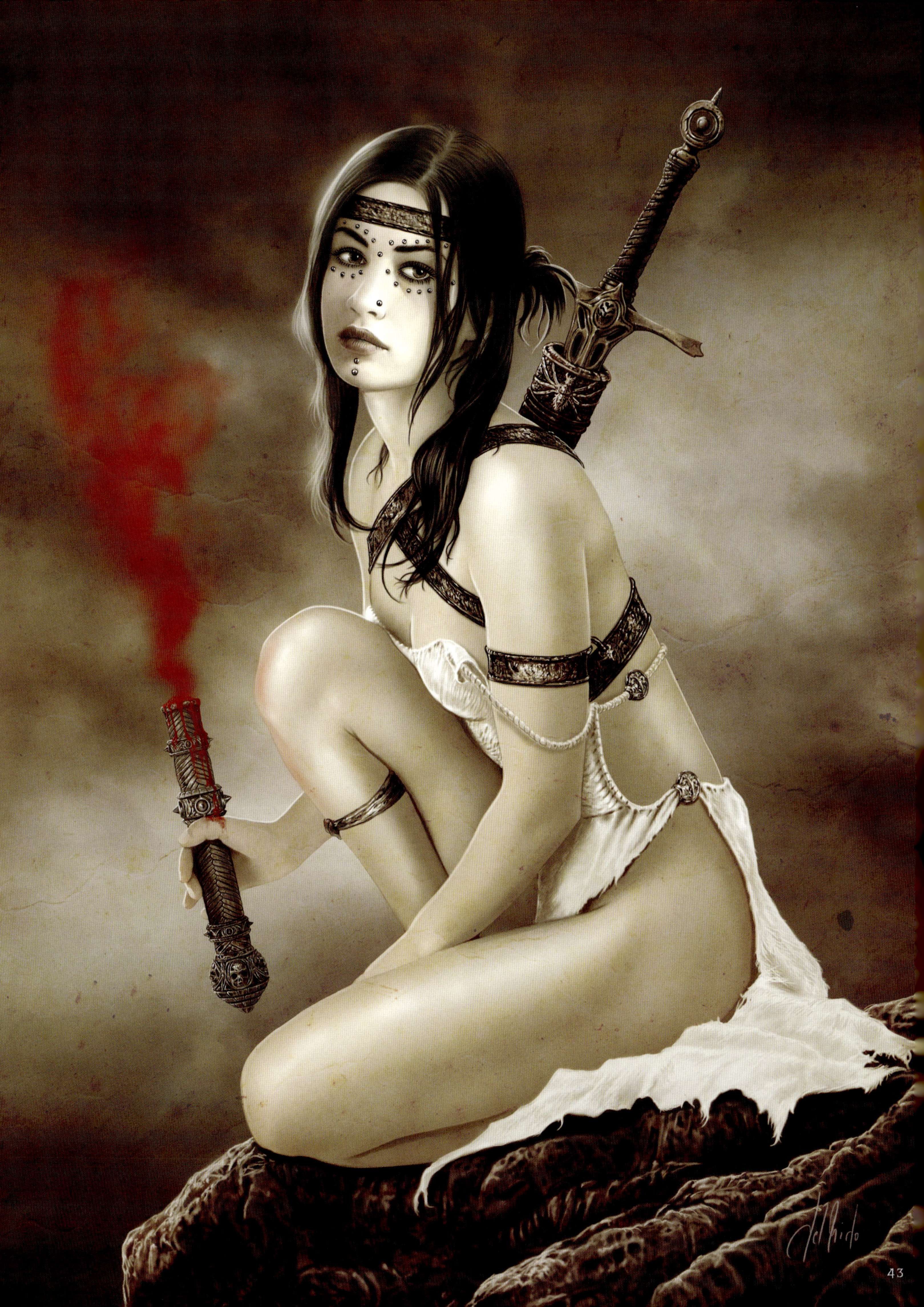

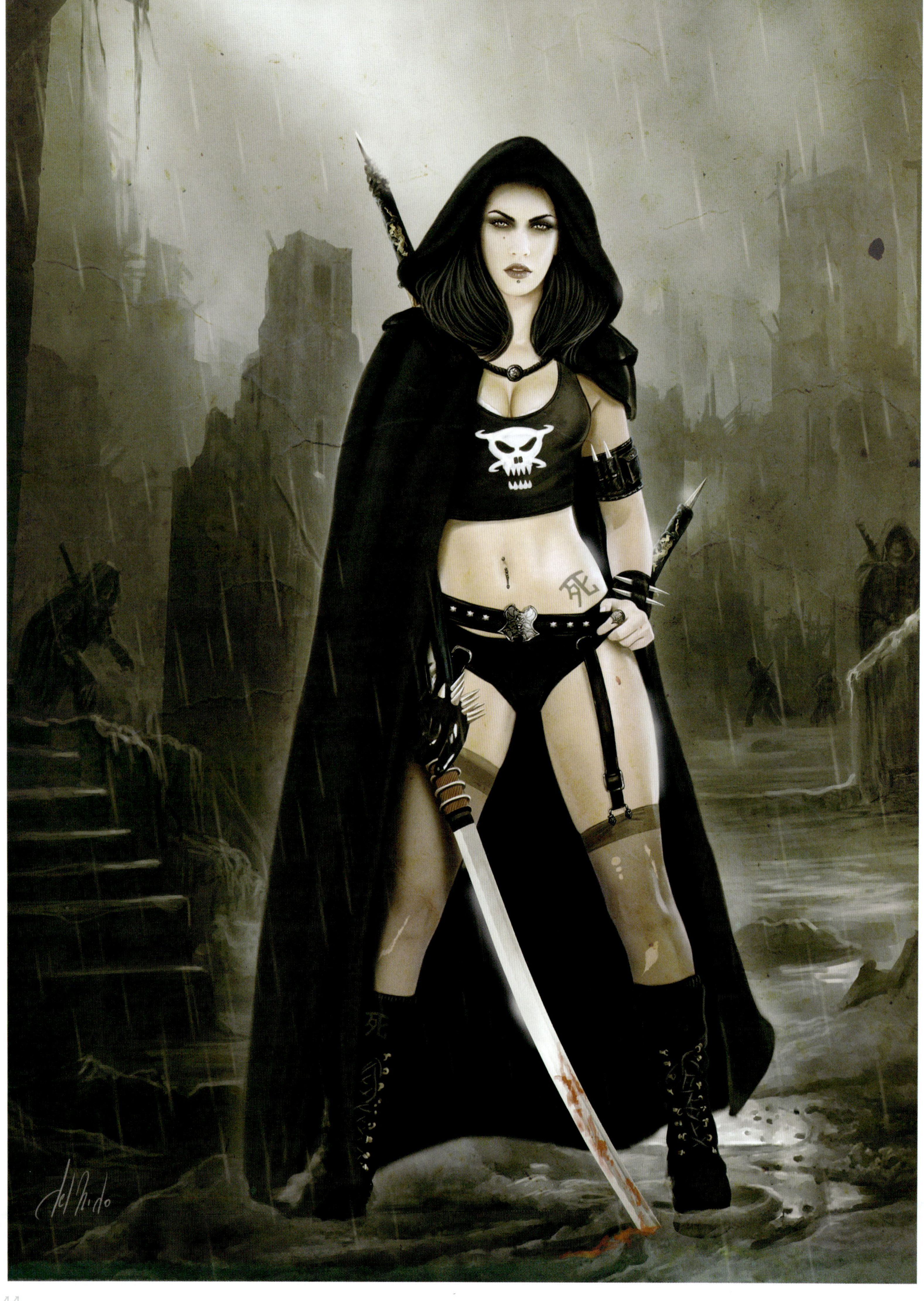

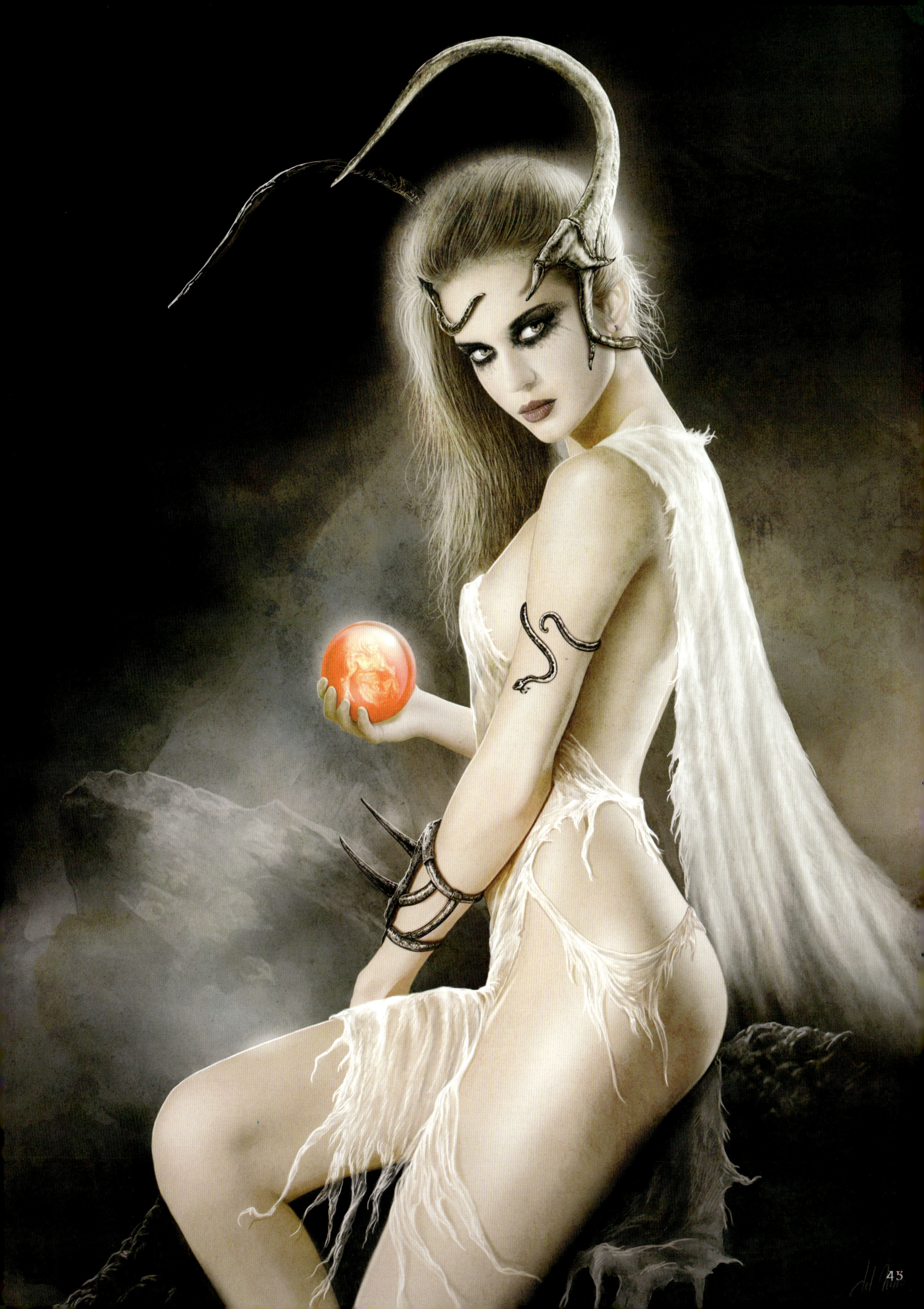

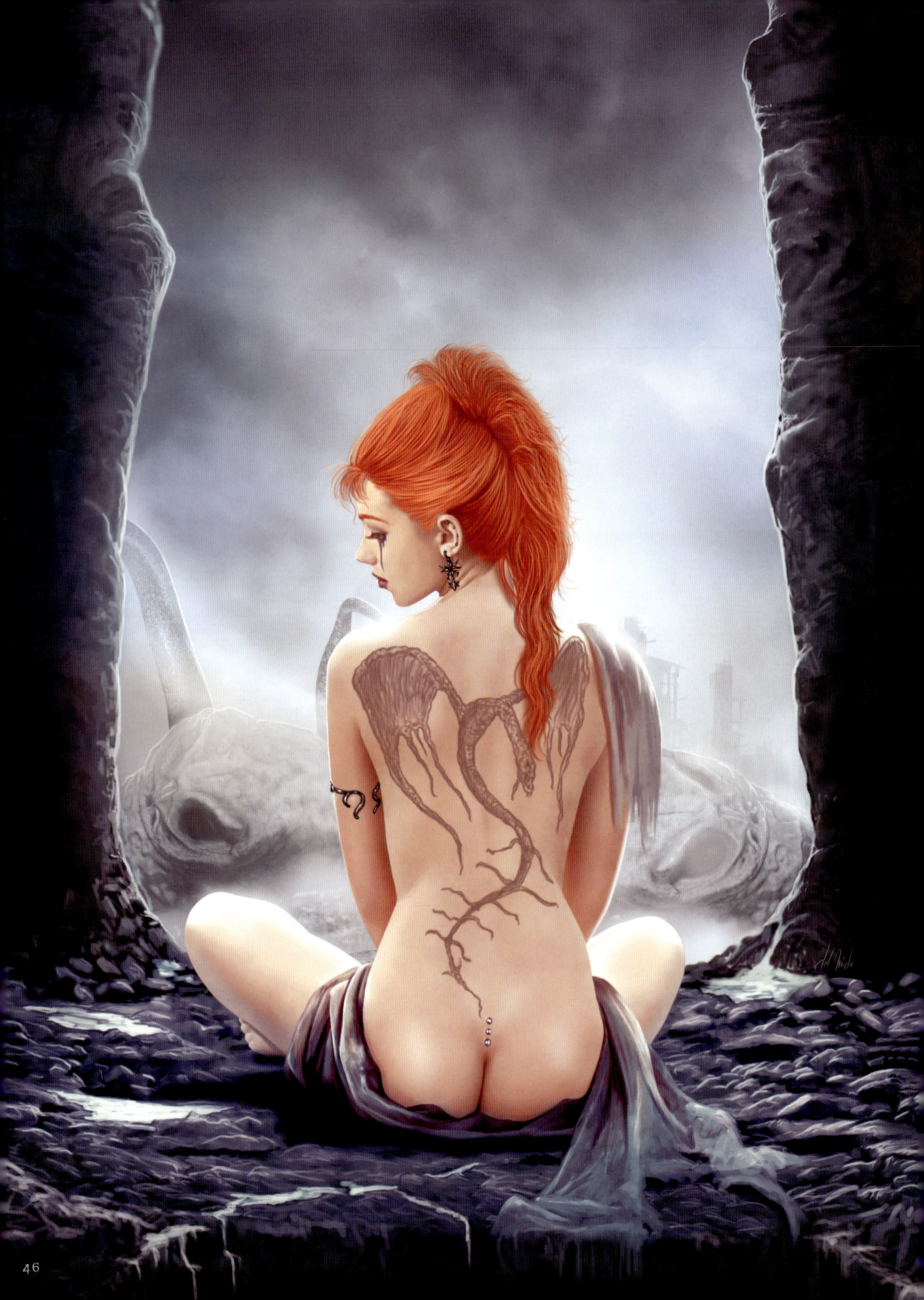

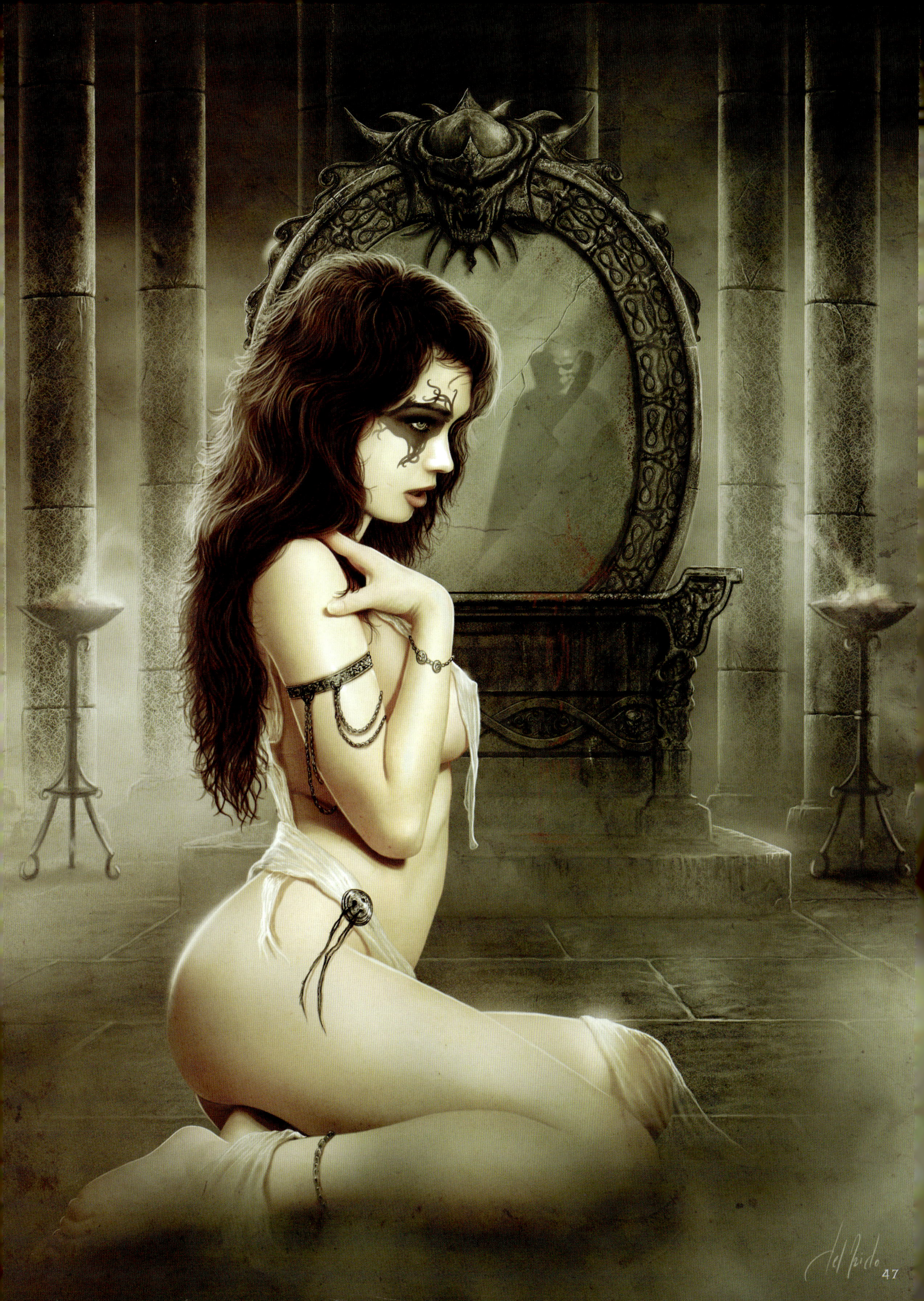

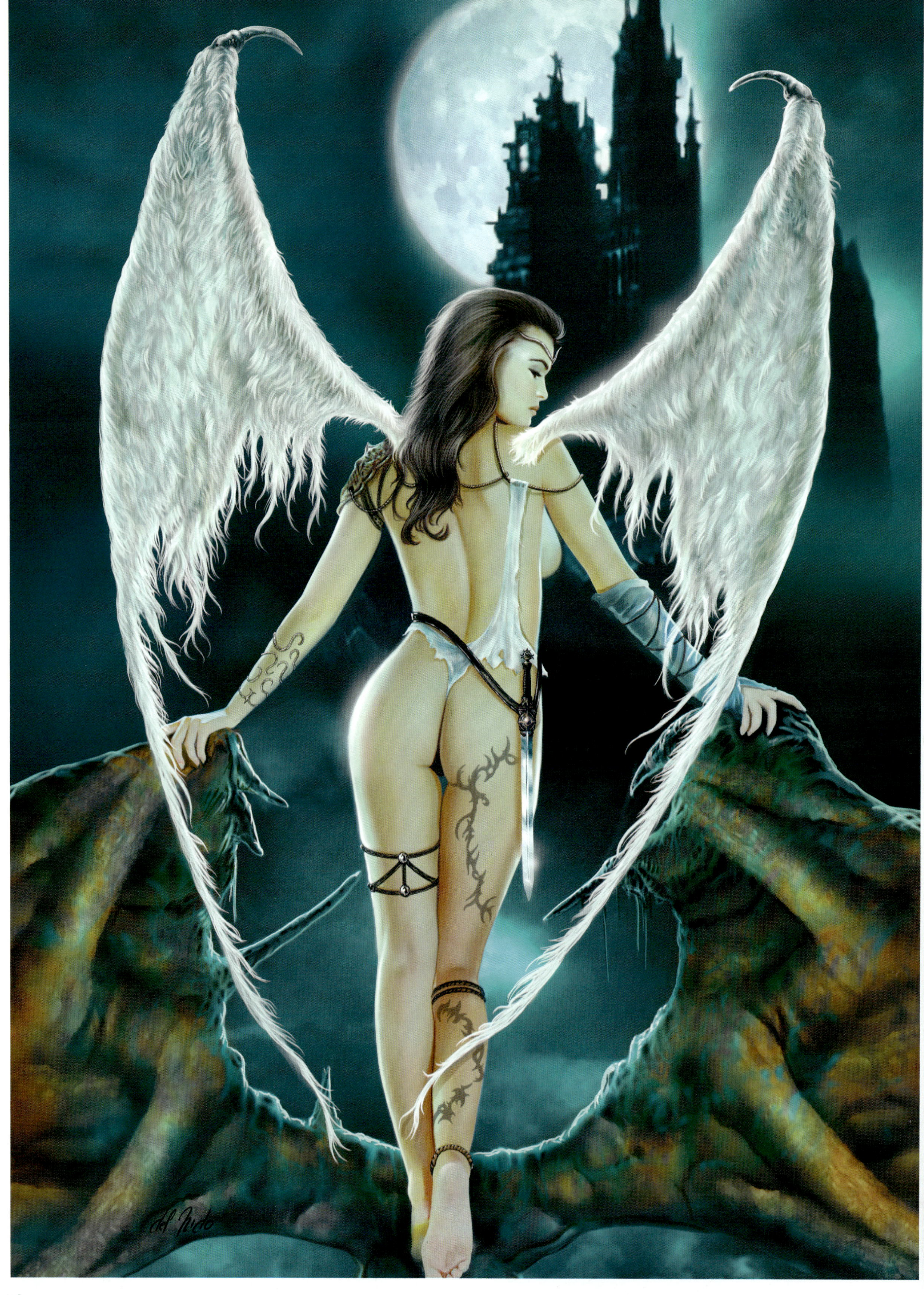